NEBUAH
What is PROPHECY?

FOUNDATION STONES

[1]

BISHOP M.
LESTER DIGHTON

Nebuah: What is Prophecy?
Series: Foundation Stones #1
© Bishop M. Lester Dighton 2025

Published by Armour Books
P. O. Box 492, Corinda QLD 4075

ISBN: 978-1-923533-03-5

Cover and interior design: Beckon Creative
Cover images:
Aaron Burden | Unsplash, 'Open book on glass table';
Arthit_Longwilai | iStock, 'One White Dove freedom flying Wings on sunset wide sky background. Symbol of International Day of Peace, Holy Spirit of God in Christian religion heaven concept'; Depositphotos | kzwwsko, 'The texture of the walls of flat granite stones, stone background'

A catalogue record for this book is available from the National Library of Australia

All rights reserved. No part of this publication may be reproduced, stored in, or introduced into a retrieval system, or transmitted, in any form, or by any means (electronic, mechanical, photocopying, recording or otherwise) without the prior written permission of the publisher.

Please note: Australian spelling, punctuation and grammar are used throughout this book.

All Scripture quotations are taken from the King James Version of the Bible. Public domain.

ACKNOWLEDGEMENTS

I would like to acknowledge my wonderful wife, Anne, for all her support and the encouragement that she constantly gives to me, for that is greatly appreciated.

I would also like to thank my friends who have given me support and encouragement, especially my friend and author of many years, now deceased, Patrick Zegenhagen, and those who contributed to this work by way of checking the details.

There are others whom have given me assistance in compiling this work, too many to name, including my students over time, and those to whom I was a student.

Of course, no acknowledgement would be complete without acknowledging the One God: Our Father in Heaven; His Son, Our Lord Jesus Christ, and the Holy Spirit who brings us into all Truth.

Thank you all, and may God Bless you.

CONTENTS

	Introduction	7
1.	What is Prophecy?	23
2.	What is a Christian?	73
3.	The End of Prophecy	95
	By the Same Author	137

INTRODUCTION

This topic emerged out of a series of talks and Bible Studies I used to conduct. At one church, we used to do talks on Prophecy towards the end of the service after the main Sermon, on a rotating roster with myself and the Bishop. (This before I was consecrated as Bishop myself). On top of this, I used to conduct Bible Studies around these topics every week, and continued for some years. As always, there were some who thoroughly enjoyed them, and wanted more. However, there was also a lot of opposition to teaching Prophecy at all.

I have been asked by various people WHY there is a need to teach such things? Is it even necessary? And do you mind becoming so educated like this?

Some of the questions are of good quality, while some are not, but they are all to be addressed, for they are of obvious concern to some people. I will now give my answers to these, and thus give you opportunity to answer them yourselves.

OUR CALLING:

'Go ye therefore, and teach all nations, baptising them in the name of the Father, and of the Son, and of the Holy Ghost: teaching them to observe all things whatsoever I have commanded you: and, lo, I am with you always, even unto the end of the world. AMEN.'

Matthew 28:19–20

THE REASON:

'My people are destroyed for lack of knowledge.'

Hosea 4:6

They are **not** just 'made sick' but actually destroyed! If that is not a call to action, and for teaching, then what is? This is why we need to teach such things, so that you **may not perish for lack** of knowledge of God, and His Commandments.

God's Answer:

'...and I will give you pastors according to Mine heart, which shall feed you with knowledge and understanding.'

Jeremiah 3:15

The Outcome:

'...and wisdom and knowledge shall be the stability of thy times, and strength of salvation: the fear of the Lord is His treasure.'

Isaiah 33:6

I will now give you with a passage from Colossians 1:9–15, for you to think about.

*⁹ '...for this cause we also, since the day we heard it, do not cease to pray for you, and to desire **that ye might be***

> ***FILLED** with the knowledge of His Will** in all **wisdom and spiritual understanding**;*
> *¹⁰ that ye may walk worthy of the Lord unto all pleasing, being faithful in every good work, and **increasing in the knowledge of God**;*
> *¹¹ strengthened with all might, according to His glorious power, unto all patience and longsuffering with joyfulness;*
> *¹² giving thanks unto the Father, which hath made us meet to be partakers of the inheritance of the saints in light:*
> *¹³ who hath delivered us from the power of darkness, and hath translated us into the kingdom of His dear Son:*
> *¹⁴ in whom we have redemption through His blood, even the forgiveness of sins:*
> *¹⁵ who is the image of the invisible God, the firstborn of every creature.'*
>
> *(Emphases mine)*
>
> *And I fell at his feet to worship him. And he said unto me, See thou do it not: I am thy fellowservant, and of thy brethren that have the testimony of Jesus: worship*

God: ***for the testimony of Jesus is the spirit of prophecy***.

Revelation 19:10

Naturally, there are many more Bible passages than these, and why not look at some of these as part of a Bible Study at home yourself?

I am often amazed and clearly dismayed at the enormous disparity between what one would expect Christians, who have spent an entire lifetime going to Church and listening to the sermons, to know, against what they actually do know. Add to this the many Bible Studies attended, and one would think that the knowledge base would be substantial, but it is not the case. WHY?

One conclusion has to be the quality of teaching they are receiving. Yes, I know that there will always be some not able to absorb it readily, but that does not cover the spread of the situation throughout all people as seen in all the churches today. They do not understand even the basics, and when you try to add to it, they wonder what you are doing. None of the others do that, so why should you? I find this an appalling attitude. IF we love God, then why not get to know Him?

Nebuah

Surely, when we love someone, we would want to know something of them. Even if we just think we love them, we do this—and yet, when it comes to God, we shy away. WHY? Sadly, this goes for the Teachers of The Word just as much, and so we get taught very little, especially little of value to us in our standing with God. Naturally, there is a spiritual aspect to this, and it is a big factor, but God has given us victory over this if we choose to use it!

As Babes

We are told in 1 Corinthians 3:2 —

I have fed you with milk, and not with meat: for hitherto ye were not able to bear it, neither yet now are ye able.

This shows that when we are babes in our walk with God, we need to be fed on milk for we cannot stand meat. We see this principle everywhere around us, for God has written it into His Creation for us to learn from, but—and this is a **big** BUT—we should grow up and start eating meat at some point in time. As it says in Hebrews 5:12 —

For when for the time ye ought to be teachers, ye have need that one teach you again which be the first principles of the oracles of God; and are become such as have need of milk, and not of strong meat.

When the time has come for us to be TEACHERS, we are still babes on milk needing to be taught all over again even the first principles. We should be the TEACHERS, but we are not. Sadly, this is just so true for most of professing Christianity in the world today. After so much time spent in churches and Bible Studies, we should be TEACHERS in the world, and not just TEACHERS, but *GOOD* TEACHERS. However, we are nowhere close to that. What a damning testimony against us!

It clarifies and demonstrates this more in the next verse, Hebrews 5:13 —

For every one that useth milk is unskilful in the word of righteousness: for he is a babe.

Unskilful is a sad indictment against us who are charged with bearing the Good News to the world. Do you think that the Great Commission to go and teach all nations is only for a select few? No! It is for all of us, each and every one, and just what do you think God is going to say to you on Judgement Day when He asks you why you didn't do it?

Another aspect to being 'babes' on milk is to do with *emotional* 'Altar Calls' (as opposed to *rational*), which produces *'premature'* babies in Christ (for they come in too early, and for the wrong reasons), and these are then a burden on the resources of the churches. They need milk and care from other church members for far too long, just to survive. Yes, it is nice to have people give their lives to Christ—don't get me wrong on that—but we are to be sure they are ready to give their lives to Christ, and make informed choices on what they believe, rather than just on emotional responses to a service or to a charismatic speaker.

DUTY AND DECEPTION

Teaching—that is, spreading God's Word—is a duty of *all* Christians, and one which we should be conducting on a regular basis to those around us. This is especially true if it is teaching straight out of the Scriptures, but tempered to the needs of the person in question, and only the Holy Spirit can guide us in that. Naturally, some are going to be better at it than others, but that *never* removes the duty involved for all. Some are going to be gifted at it, and this is in accordance with God's Word: 1 Corinthians 12 and Ephesians 4 are good places to see that.

Are you one of the group condemned in Scripture, firstly in:

And have not obeyed the voice of my teachers, nor inclined mine ear to them that instructed me!

Proverbs 5:13

Ye who turn judgment to wormwood, and leave off righteousness in the earth, seek Him that maketh the seven stars and Orion, and turneth the shadow of death into the morning, and maketh the day dark with night: that calleth for the waters of the sea, and poureth them out upon the face of the earth: The LORD is His name: that strengtheneth the spoiled against the strong, so that the spoiled shall come against the fortress. They hate him that rebuketh in the gate, and they abhor him that speaketh uprightly. Forasmuch

Nebuah

> *therefore as your treading is upon the poor, and ye take from him burdens of wheat: ye have built houses of hewn stone, but ye shall not dwell in them; ye have planted pleasant vineyards, but ye shall not drink wine of them. For I know your manifold transgressions and your mighty sins: they afflict the just, they take a bribe, and they turn aside the poor in the gate from their right.*
>
> Amos 5:7–12

And then in Paul's letter to Timothy, where we see:

> *For the time will come when they will not endure sound doctrine; but after their own lusts shall they heap to themselves teachers, having itching ears; and they shall turn away their ears from the truth, and shall be turned unto fables.*
>
> 2 Timothy 4:3–4

and

> *Now go, write it before them in a table, and note it in a book, that it may be for the time to come for ever and ever: That this is a rebellious people, lying children,*

children that will not hear the law of the LORD: which say to the seers, See not; and to the prophets, Prophesy not unto us right things, speak unto us smooth things, prophesy deceits: Get you out of the way, turn aside out of the path, cause the Holy One of Israel to cease from before us.

Wherefore thus saith the Holy One of Israel, Because ye despise this word, and trust in oppression and perverseness, and stay thereon.

Isaiah 30:8–12

I can only pray that you are not willingly part of this group, but there is another group which we are subject to, and they are equally condemned by God:

Thy first father hath sinned, and thy teachers have transgressed against Me.

Isaiah 43:27

Now turn to:

But there were false prophets also among the people, even as there shall be false teachers among you, who privily shall bring in damnable heresies, even

> *denying the Lord that bought them, and bring upon themselves swift destruction. And many shall follow their pernicious ways; by reason of whom the way of truth shall be evil spoken of. And through covetousness shall they with feigned words make merchandise of you: whose judgment now of a long time lingereth not, and their damnation slumbereth not.*
>
> 2 Peter 2:1–3

> *For there are many unruly and vain talkers and deceivers, specially they of the circumcision: Whose mouths must be stopped, who subvert whole houses, teaching things which they ought not, for filthy lucre's sake.*
>
> Titus 1:10–11

Sadly, too many who are 'teachers' of God's Word do not know this enough, and this is not all, for we see it in:

> *From which some having swerved have turned aside unto vain jangling; desiring to be teachers of the law;*

understanding neither what they say, nor whereof they affirm.

> 1 Timothy 1:6–7

There are also many more Bible passages on this subject, e.g., Psalm 50:16–23.

Beware of them

It tells us in plain language that such teachers do not understand just what they are teaching, and so bring in all sorts of damnable heresies. Some do so intentionally, and they will surely answer for that on Judgement Day, but in the meantime, they are destroying us—God's Children, and they are slated for swift destruction for it! **Beware of them!**

The only way to tell just who is who, is to get into God's Word and *compare their actions to what the Word tells us they should be teaching and doing*—each and every time they speak as a spokesperson of God.

OF FULL AGE

What a clear and stark contrast to what we saw in Colossians 1:9–15! Are we going to be content to be babies all our lives, or are we going to grow up and take responsibility?

> *But strong meat belongeth to them that are of full age, even those who by reason of use have their senses exercised to discern both good and evil.*
>
> Hebrews 5:14

Are we going to get into God's Word and see for ourselves the treasures within, or are we going to let the enemy win, and destroy our chance to get into Heaven as a result? Will you throw away the PEARL OF GREAT PRICE that the Lord God has for you? Will you be a Jeremiah 3:15 sort of person and reap the outcome as listed in Isaiah 33:6?

How about this passage:

> *¹ And I saw a new heaven and a new earth: for the first heaven and the first earth were passed away; and there was no more sea. ² And I John saw the holy*

city, new Jerusalem, coming down from God out of heaven, prepared as a bride adorned for her husband. ³ And I heard a great voice out of heaven saying, Behold, the tabernacle of God is with men, and He will dwell with them, and they shall be His people, and God Himself shall be with them, and be their God. ⁴ And God shall wipe away all tears from their eyes; and there shall be no more death, neither sorrow, nor crying, neither shall there be any more pain: for the former things are passed away. ⁵ And He that sat upon the throne said, Behold, I make all things new. And He said unto me, Write: for these words are true and faithful. ⁶ And He said unto me, It is done. I am Alpha and Omega, the beginning and the end. I will give unto him that is athirst of the fountain of the water of life freely. ⁷ He that overcometh shall inherit all things; and I will be his God, and he shall be My son.

Revelation 21:1–7

Even the Secularists recognise that one needs to set goals, and where you set those goals is where you will usually end up. Is this the sort of place where you would like to end up, and, if so, is this your goal? If this is your goal, then it also requires the asking of if you are working towards it, for this is where the Mature Christians will certainly end up!

Here is something to think about:

> *There is an abundance of gold and precious stones,* ***but lips of knowledge are a rare jewel****.*
>
> Proverbs 20:15

Are you willing to be a rare jewel for the Lord?

Your choice —
'SMOKING' or 'NON-SMOKING'
for Eternity!

Which one will you choose, and where will you end up?

1

WHAT IS PROPHECY?

BIBLE READINGS:

1 John 4:1–7
1 Corinthians 14:1–8
Matthew 24:24

¹ Beloved, believe not every spirit, but try the spirits whether they are of God: because many false prophets are gone out into the world. ² Hereby know ye the Spirit of God: Every spirit that confesseth that Jesus Christ is come in the flesh is of God: ³ And every spirit that confesseth not that Jesus Christ is come in the flesh is not of God: and this is that spirit of antichrist, whereof ye have heard that it should come; and even now already is it in the world. ⁴ Ye are of God, little children, and have overcome them: because greater is he that is in you, than he that is in the world. ⁵ They are of the world: therefore speak they of the world, and the world heareth them. ⁶ We are of God: he that knoweth God heareth us; he that is not of God heareth not us. Hereby know we the spirit of truth, and the spirit of error. ⁷ Beloved, let us love one another: for love is of God; and every one that loveth is born of God, and knoweth God.

1 John 4:1–7

¹ Follow after charity, and desire spiritual gifts, but rather that ye may prophesy. ² For he that speaketh in an unknown tongue speaketh not unto men, but unto God: for no man understandeth him; howbeit in the spirit he speaketh mysteries. ³ But he that prophesieth speaketh unto men to edification, and exhortation, and comfort. ⁴ He that speaketh in an unknown tongue edifieth himself; but he that prophesieth edifieth the church. ⁵ I would that ye all spake with tongues, but rather that ye prophesied: for greater is he that prophesieth than he that speaketh with tongues, except he interpret, that the church may receive edifying. ⁶ Now, brethren, if I come unto you speaking with tongues, what shall I profit you, except I shall speak to you either by revelation, or by knowledge, or by prophesying, or by doctrine? ⁷ And even things without life giving sound, whether pipe or harp, except they give a distinction in the sounds, how shall it be known what is piped or harped? ⁸ For if the trumpet give an uncertain sound, who shall prepare himself to the battle?

1 Corinthians 14:1–8

For there shall arise false Christs, and false prophets, and shall shew great signs and wonders; insomuch that, if it were possible, they shall deceive the very elect.

Matthew 24:24

So, what **is** 'PROPHECY'?

Now, I know that this is a HUGE subject, and even when I was teaching Bible Studies, I taught more than 35 keys to understanding Prophecy in Scripture, which took more than 12 months, even with the more dedicated students. However, as the Lord increases my understanding and wisdom in these things, I feel I may have to add more yet, so it could easily become too big a task for here. However, we need to put some foundations in place, for, as the Lord said through Hosea the prophet:

> *My people are destroyed for lack of knowledge!*
>
> Hosea 4:6

So, here is a sermon (with a few minor clarifications) I did on this:

There are many ASPECTS to Prophecy, from 'Foretelling' to 'Forth-telling'; from 'History' as Prophecy, to 'Scriptural Truth' as Prophecy; the 'Office of a Prophet' versus the 'Gift of Prophecy' versus an 'Instance of Prophecy', and so on; none of which I am going to cover today, not even anything on the Gifts. We are only building foundations today.

SO, WHAT IS 'PROPHECY'?

Apart from being something that is overly ABUSED by modern scholars and churches today, that is. Is it these things that just pop into your mind and therefore must be fully true ... *or not?* Is it foretelling the future by any means, or is it something specific? Is it going to the local tarot card reader, or the tea-house to see what the leaves say, or is it found elsewhere? *Is* it found in some of those who claim to be 'Prophets' and 'Men of God' that we see on the TV? We will see more on how to gauge this. Is it reading your stars in the local newspaper?

Let us go back into Scripture to see something of prophecy there but, I must warn you that, even though I will only give some basics as a foundation, you may well be challenged in your current approach to God, for many False Prophets are already deceiving us today. However, there is a flip-side to that, for there are also GOOD *'People of God'* who only wish to lead us to God's Holy

Kingdom for Eternity, and that is why we need to know what Prophecy *is* ... and *isn't!*

The word 'Prophet' first appears back in Genesis 20, and then appears regularly right through Scripture, until we see it often in Revelation. However, in 1 Samuel 9:9, we see the first usage historically:

> *Beforetime in Israel, when a man went to enquire of God, thus he spake, Come, and let us go to the* SEER: *for he that is now called a Prophet was beforetime called a* SEER.

The dictionaries tell us that a Seer is 'someone who sees' for whatever reason, while a Prophet is 'an inspired person', but nothing is told to us of 'by whom', and 'for what reason'.

In the passage that follows this verse, we see some pretty clear descriptions of the methodology of a Prophet, but first, let me set the stage as it's described in the earlier verses of the chapter:

> *And he had a son, whose name was Saul, a choice young man, and a goodly: and there was not among the children of*

Israel a goodlier person than he: from his shoulders and upward he was higher than any of the people. And the asses of Kish, Saul's father were lost. And Kish said to Saul his son, Take now one of the servants with thee, and arise, go seek the asses. And he passed through mount Ephraim, and passed through the land of Shalisha, but they found them not: then they passed through the land of Shalim, and there they were not: and he passed through the land of the Benjamites, but they found them not.

1 Samuel 9:2–4

OK, now that we have done that, it is time to continue. Let's skip over to verse 15:

[15] Now the LORD had told Samuel in his ear a day before Saul came, saying, [16] Tomorrow about this time I will send thee a man out of the land of Benjamin, and thou shalt anoint him to be captain over My people Israel, that he may save My people out of the hand of the Philistines: for I have looked upon My people, because their cry is come unto Me. [17] And when

Samuel saw Saul, the Lord *said unto him, Behold the man whom I spake to thee of! this same shall reign over My people.*

[18] Then Saul drew near to Samuel in the gate, and said, Tell me, I pray thee, where the seer's house is. [19] And Samuel answered Saul, and said, I am the seer: go up before me unto the high place; for ye shall eat with me today, and tomorrow I will let thee go, and will tell thee all that is in thine heart. [20] And as for thine asses that were lost three days ago, set not thy mind on them; for they are found. And on whom is all the desire of Israel? Is it not on thee, and on all thy father's house?

[21] And Saul answered and said, Am not I a Benjamite, of the smallest of the tribes of Israel? and my family the least of all the families of the tribe of Benjamin? wherefore then speakest thou so to me? [22] And Samuel took Saul and his servant, and brought them into the parlour, and made them sit in the chiefest place among them that were bidden, which were about thirty persons. [23] And Samuel said unto the

cook, Bring the portion which I gave thee, of which I said unto thee, Set it by thee. [24] And the cook took up the shoulder, and that which was upon it, and set it before Saul. And Samuel said, Behold that which is left! set it before thee, and eat: for unto this time hath it been kept for thee since I said, I have invited the people. So Saul did eat with Samuel that day.

1 Samuel 9:15–24

What is very clear here is the depth of detail; the *who, when, where,* and *why,* are all clearly outlined.

There is none of that vague calling: *'there is someone who is getting older'* or *'there is someone who has a mother and father'*, or even *'there is someone with a bad back'*!

What a contrast to how God's Prophets work! Anyone who works like that needs to be challenged, for the Scriptures tell us:

Beloved, believe not every spirit, but try the spirits whether they are of God:

> *because many false prophets are gone out into the world.*
>
> 1 John 4:1

Later on, we will cover some things to look for to 'Try the Spirits'. I will give a clue here though, and it is this: Does it align properly with the Word of God? This is the first and mightiest clue. With this, I do understand that, occasionally, this 'vagueness' is necessary for some reason, but should NEVER be the core, or sole, method used, as so often seen these days.

Before we continue, I wish to address another aspect of this vagueness, and one which is a major problem that is showing up everywhere today, and that is: *'God has a calling on your life.'* You see and hear this so often in various Churches today and it is a real problem! You see many energetic and enthusiastic people claiming the *role* of the Prophet. Yet this is without Discernment. They make pronouncement after pronouncement—all with good intentions. Yes, God does indeed have a calling on these people that they speak to. However, just what that calling is, is so rarely specified. Often it is something entirely different to what they are being led to do by these *'prophets'*.

Your calling MAY be to teach and preach, but it may also be to clean toilets for the service of the whole community, or to cook for the homeless. There are a myriad of things that need doing other than being up front on the platform or the pulpit, and God can be calling you to fill any of those positions, for He knows that it all needs doing. Sadly, far too many who receive a 'prophetic word' then go on to think that God is surely calling them off to the nearest seminary or Bible college to study for the next few years and, all the while, the job they were called to do goes unattended. Their homelife suffers as they try to pay for the studies, for it does not have the backing of what God wants for them. The problems continue to grow when we see them up preaching, for that is not their gifting or calling, and so we see poor quality teaching, and even poorer-run churches.

All of this because they were not told just what their calling was—specifically. Today, we can see so many churches losing their leaders as they realise that they just cannot go on in this way. They are beginning to realise that the pulpit was not their real destination, nor was it their calling under God. All of this happens because the *'prophet'* did not do their job properly.

Every time a prophet speaks for God, then it should point to God, through His Son, Jesus Christ, and not to the will of any man. It should be all about how we are to best serve Our Lord and maker, not on how WE would want it to be for our own glory and vanity. Now, don't get me wrong, for there really ARE some who are called to be up front at the Pulpit, and Preaching and Teaching with real power from God, but not everyone is so called.

Can you see the hand of the enemy in this, creating division and strife? I can. Fortunately, there are some who do get it right, so do not throw out everything that is given in Church in this way. However, make sure that it is independently confirmed outside of these people before acting upon it. God always gives—and then *confirms*—when it is His Will for us.

We also see a couple of *aspects* of 'Prophecy' in this passage in the book of Samuel. Now not only did Samuel see AHEAD of time to *who* and *what*, but we also see that he saw this in CURRENT time, to know *why* these men were there (looking for the asses). In other words, Prophecy here is shown to not only be about the FUTURE, but also the PRESENT. Are there any other indicators in

Scripture that show this aspect? Of course, the answer is 'yes'.

Let us look at Jesus Himself. We know how He often foretold of what was to happen to Him in the FUTURE, and also declared what would happen to those around him. He accurately foretold, in reference to the Temple, that there would be *'not one stone left upon another'* in Matthew 24 for an example.

We also see that the Pharisees and people around Him knew Him to be a Prophet because He knew what was in their hearts *right then*, and even knew Him to be a prophet for what was done by Him in the present. (Matthew 14:5; 21:11, 46; Luke 7:16, 26; John 7:40, 9:17.)

This then raises the question of the past! Do we have any suggestions about prophecy covering the PAST? Of course, the answer is still *'yes'*. In this Samuel passage, we hear God speaking in the PAST tense about the plight of His people. In John 4:19, we again see Jesus being identified as a Prophet, for He knew her PAST, as well as her present situation! This is the story of the Samaritan woman at the well.

So, we see Biblical Prophecy accurately covering 'Past, Present, and Future', and not just *'you will win something someday,'* or *'you will do great things for God.'* This accurately ties in with the TRUE definition of Prophecy which, when you see what the definition in Scripture says, will explain all. Yes, The Bible DOES tell us *exactly* what Prophecy is, and, so we now turn to Revelation, Chapter 19, and go to the second part of the 10th verse:

> *I am thy fellowservant, and of thy brethren that have the testimony of Jesus: worship God: for the testimony of Jesus is the spirit of prophecy.*
>
> Revelation 19:10

Herein lies the Truth of Prophecy: <u>*the Testimony of Jesus;* the Lord and Saviour</u>, who, according to Hebrews 13:8 is:

> *Jesus Christ the same yesterday, and today, and forever.*

Due to the FACT of our Lord Jesus Christ being the same yesterday, today, and forever, and the FACT that prophecy is the Testimony of Him, then of course Prophecy is about the Past, Present, and the Future—all at the same time!

Back in the reading from 1 Corinthians 14:4 it states that *'but he that prophesieth edifieth the church.'* Yet again, this is because anyone who gives the TESTIMONY of our Lord Jesus Christ, who is the Spirit of Prophecy, edifies *His* Church!

By the way, for those who do not know what the word 'edify' means, it is to *raise up; to build up; to strengthen; to give confirmation to*—His Church.

There are so many aspects of Prophecy that seem to vary in their fulfillment and timing, and this is important also. This serves to contest and remove the concepts of 'Fatalism', 'Determinism', and of 'Dualism' that have crept into the thinking of so many—even the Jews.

God is NOT inflexible and unmoving in everything, nor does He lock everything into two different sides of action—Wrath and Love only. There is little that is *'locked in'* to the extent that removes our Freewill and Choices that we make. Yes, the Final Restoration of all things is 'locked in', but there are an almost infinite ways of getting there in the time we have before then. Prophecy can aid in reaching the best outcomes under God, because all prophecy is a *'Call'* to draw closer to God.

However, little else is unalterable and definite—we can continue to make our own choices, and suffer the consequences or the benefits of each and every decision that we choose. From this, we can see the ongoing need for the 'prophet' for now.

Let us move on with our subject. Naturally, the 'voice of the prophet' cannot act alone, for it needs certain things to get it to happen at times, and the most important one of these is Prayer. Take a look at Daniel. He prayed and prayed (Daniel 9:1–19), and the Angel of The Lord came to him to *'Tell'* and to *'Give'*: to *'Explain'* and to *'Exhort'* (9:20–23). Are we praying for what God has to tell us? Are we praying to know His Will for us? Are we praying for God to assist us to live it out, each and every day? How many of us recognise that none of us came to God without someone praying for us! Do you want others to come to God also? Then pray for them! Does the Word of the Lord come to you, or even one of His Angels come to you? Do you even want it to? It can happen, you know, but you have to pray first, and last.

The 'Word of The Lord' came to men, and the exact nature of this Word is spelled out in the first part of John's Gospel:

> *In the beginning was the Word, and the Word was with God, and the Word was God.*
>
> John 1:1

This shows us that the Plan of God transcends all of time, and all of space. There is nothing that we could do that can escape the presence of God, or His Word around us, and so we need to become aware of it, and listen to it, but it has a price. We need to know what are its rules and limitations, and how does it apply to us. Let us have a quick look at this.

As God is absolute, then His Truth is absolute—100% and nothing less! Because it is 100% Truth; 10% doesn't cut it, not even 80%. Anyone who says that anything less than 100% is good enough, is serving their OWN agenda— NOT God's! As the Spirit of Prophecy is *all about this very plan God has for our Salvation for us through His Son*, Jesus of Nazareth, the Christ, the Messiah, then that makes the Word of God 100%

Prophetic, and nothing less! If we consider that Spiritual Truth is Prophecy; Types and Shadows are prophetic, and the way we act and react under God does not change, then this confirms that the Bible is 100% Prophecy.

Over the years, I have had to explain the 100% concept to a lot of people. To me, the best way of explaining it is by way of an analogy. This works for explaining Dialectics and how it destroys Truth just as easily as it explains the need for 100% in Truth, and in understanding Prophecy.

I have actually used this analogy for many years, but have only now written it down. Let us call Truth 'Dry Land', and Lies we will call 'Water', or more correctly, the 'Sea of Lies'. These symbols are right out of Scripture, in that God gave us Dry Land out of the Waters right back in Genesis 1:10, and that Our Lord and Saviour is the Rock of Ages (Dry Land), who is also the Truth, the Light, and the Way. So, if we stand on the Truth, then we are on Dry Land, but if we indulge in the Lie, then we are in deep Water. We even have a saying which says that, when we lie, we get ourselves into deep water. So, just how far do we have to be out into the Water before we are no longer standing on DRY LAND? Do we need to be over our heads and out of our depth? Maybe just chest-deep, or waist-deep, or even knee-deep? Even toe-deep is still in the WATER, and not on DRY LAND. Even 1 centimetre into the water is no longer on DRY LAND! So, there is nothing less than being 100% on DRY LAND (Truth) that is out of the WATER, and so it is with Prophecy. Only by being 100% in the Truth (on DRY LAND) is to have nothing to do with being a Lie. Anything else involves the Lie, or many Lies. Remember that the other fellow is the Father of Lies, and that is not the intent for us from God.

The Word of God is also based upon the Laws of Language, which means specific word usage, grammar, and so on. It is not just a few sounds spoken over and over again, which is supposed to mean everything from the dog is sick to God is Great. If you think that it does not matter if it is just something like a proper language, then ask Eve what happened when she only quoted *something like* the Word of God to Satan, for we see suffering pass down to this very day from then.

This clearly demonstrates that using less than 100% is not good enough! Jesus quoted the **pure**

Word of God (100%) to Satan when He was tempted, and so Satan could not win there. Far too many fail this test!

Another test of Prophecy is Accuracy. Does it come to pass exactly (100%) as said? If not, then the person is a False Prophet and, in the Old Testament, worthy to be stoned to death. Not that I am advocating that now! Their death now should be accomplished at the Cross of Jesus.

Do you now understand what Prophecy is, and isn't?

I will give an example of how to tell the difference between Seers and Prophets, for this will assist in our understanding of this subject. I was asked by a church in Brisbane to examine the works of the early twentieth century South African seer, Nicholas Van Rensburg, to know if they should teach from the book, *Voice of a Prophet*, by Adriaan Snyman (Vaandel Publishers 1999).

At first, there are clear descriptions of Riders and Battles, and you may think that this man must really be from God and one of His Prophets, as so many claim. Yet, sadly, when you apply the *criteria* to his works, then it does NOT match. Let me explain, but, of course, we should only do these things AFTER and WITH Prayer, allowing God's Holy Spirit to be our guide in this!

- Not once does he edify Christ's Church in his visions.

- Not once does he mention the Lord or His Eternal Kingdom, or Repentance, Belief, Faith, Baptism, or any of these things we know are necessary to our Christianity in his visions (and this because we are given these things in God's Holy Word to compare with).

- You see some visions being interpreted in up to five different ways to get them to fit circumstances going on. However, we are told in Scripture:

Knowing this first, that no prophecy of the scripture is of any private interpretation.

2 Peter 1:20

Yet again, we have contradiction to what is told to us as our guide in Scripture.

- Another one is Displacement (or Replacement) Theology—Boers replacing the Jews! God does not forsake the Jews, nor leave them. If He did, then the truth of Scripture would be nullified. We need to be sure of what theology we teach, for our doctrine should be grounded in God's Holy Word (100%). Displacement Theology is another area where far too many fail! Neither the Church nor any nation has replaced the people of Israel in God's plans but been grafted in.

- Yet another warning sign is that his visions are claimed to be an *addition* to Revelation, and yet, in that book, we are told:

> *For I testify unto every man that heareth the words of the prophecy of this book, If any man shall add unto these things, God shall add unto him the plagues that are written in this book.*
>
> Revelation 22:18

- On top of this, we have the accuracy and language tests.

These same criteria are what we should use to 'try the Spirits' of the television evangelists and visiting preachers, along with all others who claim to serve the Lord God. To do this properly, we need to KNOW the Scriptures, and be willing to **diligently** search them on every occasion, *with prayer*, for only this approach will lead us in Truth. We must do like the Bereans of old did.

If we get it right, then our place in Heaven is assured but, if not, then there will be *'wailing and gnashing of teeth'*, and I wish that not on any person.

Prophecy is also to warn of things, so that we do not fall into the traps of the enemy, both physically and spiritually. Van Rensburg does match the physical aspect many times, but not the spiritual. To his credit, Nicolas Van Rensburg never claimed to be a prophet, but always referred to himself as a 'seer'. It is people like US now today that call him a prophet!

I am not going to make the final call as to whether he is a Prophet or a Seer, for I do not have a copy of the 'Book of Life' to tell that. I can only test the Spirits according to Scripture. I will leave that up to you. However, what I will ask you to do is to not be deceived by false prophets who lead us to false Christs, and miss out on your opportunity to enter God's Holy Kingdom for all Eternity! We should always be mindful of that. Please read Isaiah 48, and see much more about the whys and wherefores of what Prophecy is. See also that it is NOT done in secret either.

In summary, we should remember what we are to look for in testing all things and trying the spirits.

- Does it edify Christ's Church?
- Does it do this in accordance with God's Word (100%)?
- Therefore, is the Theology and Doctrine sound (100%)?
- Does it follow the Laws of Language (100%)? God did give us our languages, and they are therefore perfect in their structure, and for good reason.
- Are the statements consistent with each other (as well as with God's Word)?
- Do the things stated/predicted come to pass—exactly as described (100%)?
- Does it warn us, or guide us back to God?

A lot of people today look only to 100% accuracy of prediction as an indicator that Prophet is from

God. They do not take into account these other criteria. But bear in mind the Lord's own words on accuracy:

> *If there arise among you a prophet, or a dreamer of dreams, and giveth thee a sign or a wonder, And the sign or the wonder come to pass, whereof he spake unto thee, saying, Let us go after other gods, which thou hast not known, and let us serve them; Thou shalt not hearken unto the words of that prophet, or that dreamer of dreams: for the LORD your God proveth you, to know whether ye love the LORD your God with all your heart and with all your soul. Ye shall walk after the LORD your God, and fear him, and keep his commandments, and obey his voice, and ye shall serve him, and cleave unto him.*
>
> Deuteronomy 13:1–4

These things will tell you if one is a Prophet, a False Prophet, or a Seer. If all lines up, then listen to it, but if not, then **reject** it!

Our Lord Jesus Christ is THE Light, THE Truth, and THE Way (100%): Prophecy is all about HIM in our lives and why, and never forget it is HE who died for us so that we may have that life abundantly!

AMEN

A DEFINITION

I had to follow up the foregoing sermon with this further sermon to finish it off. Since these additions were delivered, more questions and comments have arisen, so now I will move on to answering more about what Prophecy IS, and is NOT!

First, I still did not fully answer the question of *what is prophecy*, and I must now do so, to give a more complete definition of it.

First of all, what does the WORD PROPHET mean? It doesn't actually specifically mean *predicting the future* but it comes from the Hebrew word 'nabiy' and means *spokesman* or *speaker*. The Hebrew word for PROPHECY is 'nebuah'.

In the Greek, the word for *prophet* is 'prophētēs' and means several things. It is a *forth-* ('pro') *telling*, or *teaching* ('phētēs'), when God's Spirit solemnly declares to men or gives by inspiration, and the prophet either speaks it, or writes it down, or both. This then makes them to be *speakers, teachers* and *tellers* of God's Word, as they are inspired by the Holy Spirit.

Secondly, the prophet's *role* is the **elucidation** (the act of making clear) **of God's Word and His Will** to those who wish to know, as well as to some of those who are not so sure they want to know. The prophet explains to the church (and others) the meaning of what is written, so that those within the church may escape being lured in by the false teachings of those who would detract from God's Word. The prophet also may give direction to any individual or group regarding direction for God's purpose to be fulfilled. This fulfills the role of PREPARING us.

So many think that Prophecy is only about Doom and Gloom, and scary things, but that is never the primary objective of it. In this context, Prophecy is all about PREPARING us for what is to come so that we may be ready to deal with it when it does come, and not be led astray. It serves to prove that God really does know the beginning from the end, and has clearly told us of it so that we may be ready for it; not just in our external experiences, but our internal ones as well. The Primary Purpose is for us to Trust in God, and lean not on our own understanding. (Proverbs 3:5–7).

The scary bits of prophecy are to give us incentive to not get it wrong with God—they are to provide motivation to get it right, and are thus the secondary objective of prophecy.

Prophecy is thus **clarifying God's Will and God's Word for His purposes, and strictly according to His Will**, and <u>not that of any man</u>.

It means that **it is the express telling and/or showing us His Will in every aspect of our lives, including the Past, Present, and the Future, so that He may be glorified in us, and by us.**

THIS IS SO THAT WE MAY **DIRECT, ENCOURAGE, EXHORT** AND **COMFORT** THOSE **WHO ARE WISHING TO KNOW** ABOUT **OUR LORD GOD** IN THEIR LIVES, TO EDIFY HIS CHURCH.

Yet another definition which is mentioned in Scripture, is to **Preach Divine Wisdom**!

As always, *it should point to God and His Will through Jesus Christ for us*, and how we are to fit in with that. It means that we can now learn to see all our actions as compared to how God sees us, and how He would have us do things. Prophecy is not subject to any private interpretation of man (2 Peter 1:20), but comes from the Holy Spirit who leads and teaches us in all Truth (1 John 2:27).

As a result, the role of PROPHET is usually closely aligned with that of the TEACHER, but with the differences coming in the form of whom is being addressed, and for what reasons. (The PROPHET/MESSENGER could be aiming at one person only, or the whole world, and not the group or congregation as in TEACHER or SHEPEHRD/PASTOR).

Collectively, the prophet's role is part of a wider ministry, and is for 'the perfecting (maturing) of the saints, for the work of the ministry, and finally, for the edifying of the body of Christ'.

Finally, the message of the prophet is often **conditional**: IF bad behaviour continues, then bad things will follow, but IF they repent (come back into God's Will), then good things will follow. The outcome is thus not always as first announced, just like with Jonah at Nineveh. He announced the destruction of the city but, because of the repentance of the citizens, God was merciful to them and Jonah's declaration of judgment did not come to pass.

The Teacher also still needs the Prophet to show him if what he is teaching IS according to God's Word: *'How do I know if what I am teaching is right in God's eyes?'* **So, from this point forward, whenever you see the word PROPHECY, it means the *Showing, or Clarifying of God's Will*** to and for us. Naturally, this means the involvement of God's Holy Spirit in giving us TRUTH in all things.

Reading, and Praying upon God's Word, is thus mandatory!

The role of the Prophet is often associated with the Gift of TEACHING—while not always or necessarily being the frontline teachers themselves—since, to give us the meaning of what God has intended, we may need instruction in associated matters as well as the core material. However, the role of the Prophet is also allied with the role of the WATCHMAN. It's the Watchman's task to call out when the enemies are at the door, and more importantly to identify *who* and *how* they are attacking, and in what force! Therefore, they are also WITNESSES *for* God and WITNESSES *against* the Devil!

Too many do not understand this!

Sadly, I will often have to use the word 'Prophecy' in something of the format misused by so many. Unfortunately, although there is misunderstanding around the term, this is necessary so that we have a common ground for communication.

The next point to cover is that many believe that God is doing new things today, which are not covered in the Scriptures of old. Some state things like, 'Jesus never used a microphone to get His messages out,' and they then go on to believe that this justifies their messages of 'God writing new things into His Word.' Let us be absolutely clear on this, God has completed His Holy Word and His Holy Spirit uses this, and ONLY this, to reach His Church today! The Word of God is complete! It is bracketed at both ends with the Commandments to NOT TO ADD TO THIS BOOK or SUBTRACT FROM IT. (Deuteronomy 4:2, Revelation 22:18–19).

Anybody who has delved into mathematics will tell you that anything included within the brackets is covered by the one action over everything so included—and this means that all the Word of God is included. The question needs to be asked: 'If it is not complete, then why does God tell us NOT to add to it, nor subtract from it?'

Simply put, God is doing the same old things, only to *new people* within His Creation! The Charismatic concept of the Prophet declaring new things to the world is thus sadly mistaken. This concept of this Ministry actually tries to tell us that God got it wrong, and we need to be advised how to get it right nowadays. (I wonder who gave them the authority to tell God He was wrong? Look at 2 Timothy 2:16, and 3:1–9). I do believe that there is a Gift of Prophecy, for the Holy Spirit has to call some to clarify to the rest of us concerning God's Will (2 Peter 1:21), but that is because the rest of us aren't listening to Him. It has to be a Gift from God, for no man could know God's Will of his own accord (John 14:26), and of course, it is listed as a Gift in Romans 12:6, Ephesians 4:8–12, and 1 Corinthians 12:4–14.

What is Prophecy?

If you look at the gods of most religions, they really are just 'powerful beings', or 'beings of power' in any given area. Even Zeus suffers from the foibles of fallen mankind. There is only ONE God who is Perfect, Omnipotent, Omniscient, etc., and who knows the Beginning from the End. He is not subject to these shortcomings, and covers ALL areas and not just some facets. He is the God of the Jews and the Christians. As God knows the beginning from the end, then He can make it known to us to show that we can rely on Him in all things. God's Word has many instances where He tells us things, so that we can compare it to what is happening and see for ourselves that He is Sure.

To think that God cannot know these things means that you are denying God of the 'Right' and 'Ability' to bring this to fruition in its completeness in due course, independently of man. Either that, or you are believing that God is not Omnipotent, and cannot bring it about except by what man is doing for Him. I would suggest some serious reflection and contemplation on either of these approaches, for one or both will stop you from looking towards, and preparing for, the Second

Coming. We see this, for example, in the writings of people like Stephen Miller.

Here is a direct quote from his Introduction to *The Complete Guide to Bible Prophecy:* **'It's a waste of precious time to speculate about the end of the world.'**

In contrast, let me share a quote from Sydney Watson's book, *In the Twinkling of an Eye:* **'This same Jesus which is taken up from you into Heaven shall so came in like manner as ye have seen Him go into Heaven.'**

He paused, then went on: 'The Second Coming of Our Lord and Saviour Jesus Christ is, I believe, the central Truth to real, true Christianity at this moment, and it should be carefully, diligently studied by every converted soul. It should be comprehended as far as Scripture reveals it, and so apprehended that we should live in daily, hourly expectancy of that return. Moody, the great Evangelist, to whom the whole subject (as he tells us) was once most objectionable, upon studying the Word of God himself, in this connection, was so profoundly impressed with the insistence with which the Return of The Lord was emphasised, that he was compelled to believe in it, to preach it, saying, "It is almost the most precious truth of all the Bible. Why, one verse in thirteen throughout the New Testament is said to allude to this wondrous subject in some form or another."'

Do you see a difference in approach?

Do you see the one saying, 'Don't worry about looking, because it is a waste of precious time,' and the other saying that it is 'almost the most precious truth of all the Bible'?

What is *your* approach?

Will you deny God's ability to carry these things out just as He said He would?

Or, will you diligently search out Holy Scripture so that you are ready and not miss so momentous an event?

Will you look at history from the viewpoint of PREPARATION and WARNING? These shadows that we see can prepare us to know and recognise what to look for in its fullness when it comes. Just as the blood of bulls and lambs gave us a shadow of things to come, the fullness WAS not, and COULD not come to pass to the very letter until the 'Lamb of God' shed His Blood for us, and completed what had previously been seen only in part!

These prophecies are not just about men, but about what God is doing with men; for mankind. Let us not be like those listed in these books and in the world, who suggest on various occasions that the Prophets of God got it wrong somewhere, or maybe that it was others who wrote in their names at later dates. I pray that these people come to know the Lord God for who He is, and to repent of such ways, so that they too may enter into God's Kingdom.

Prophecy is completely about God and is thus complete, for it comes from, and is about, a complete God. Some however question where it says that it is complete. To answer this, we must go to Revelation 10:7, but especially 1 Corinthians 13:10, where we read that it will come to an end as a result of being complete.

I am not going to cover the End of Prophecy here and now, for there is more to look at yet, but will finish this at the end of the work, for that is where that part belongs, and is better suited to our understanding if we leave this until then.

Naturally, the part of Prophecy coming to an End belongs at the 'end' of any book on Prophecy.

The final questions on this are:

- Are we willing to hear from a Prophet of God over a false prophet?
- Are we willing to follow all the way to the Kingdom of God?

We will also look at this theme more closely as we go along.

In this, I am not claiming to be the Prophet of God, for I ask these same questions of myself, but am only giving that which I have been given to share.

Is this something to know?

Of course, the questions and comments kept coming in, long after I delivered these sermons as I continued to preach about Prophecy. So, this is the next section of answering questions regarding the need for teaching on Prophecy.

Christ is the Alpha and the Omega; the Beginning and the End; which was, which is, and which is to come. We've heard this ever so many times, at least once during our Church Life, or at least I hope so. It doesn't matter how many times you hear it, unless you ponder on it prayerfully, it will never mean much to you. In our Christian focus, we teach for you to look at Christ and His Ministry as it was nearly 2000 years ago, and also to watch for His Return, but I need for you to question if this is *all* we should be considering?

Remember this: for it goes all the way back to the beginning, so let us look at it back in the beginning:

> *In the beginning **God** CREATED the heaven and the earth. And the earth was without form, and void; and darkness was upon the face of the deep. And the SPIRIT of God moved upon the face of the waters. And God said, Let there be LIGHT: and there was light.*
>
> Genesis 1:1–3

*In the beginning **God**:* So, we see right there in the beginning—God. The word used here is 'Elohim', which is a word of plurality, meaning more than one part (actually, three or more), and so we must ask if these parts are identified? The answer is, of course, yes!

Verse one tells us that He created, so the first part is the *Creator:* God. We are all familiar with The Lord God being the Creator, and so there is no further need to identify Him.

Verse two tells us that there is a *Spirit.* There are extensive verses mentioning and describing the Spirit of God, whom is Truth.

> *This is He that came by water and blood, even Jesus Christ; not by water only, but by water and blood.* ***And it is the Spirit that beareth witness****,* BECAUSE THE SPIRIT IS TRUTH.
>
> 1 John 5:6

In our translations, we see Him being called the Holy Spirit, the Holy Ghost, and the Spirit of God, and all are talking about the one thing/person/spirit.

Verse three tells us that there is *Light.* We have this 'Light' identified for us in later passages such as 1 Corinthians 8:6. He is known as the Light (John

8:12), the Word (John 1:1), the Image of God (2 Corinthians 4:4), and so many more titles yet.

So, we have **the *Creator*, the *Spirit*, and the *Light* clearly identified as the parts of this 'Elohim' that we are *'made in the image'* thereof.**

Therefore, from this, if Christ was with God *'in the Beginning'*, then should not we be considering Christ ALL the way back to the beginning? If Christ is with God *'at the End of all these things'*, shouldn't we consider the Christ ALL the way forward to the 'End of the Ages'? It needs pointing out that to only focus on one area as being important and disregard the rest, not only gives an unbalanced and biased viewpoint, it could also declare that the rest is of NO importance! This is a narrow and self-centred approach that fits in with Satan's plan of achieving 'Deification of Man' (exactly equal to Satan's own condemned opinion that he could be as God (Isaiah 14:12–15), and should be carefully avoided. Instead, it is the study of, and hopefully the careful study of Christ in *every* Age and Facet *(the same, yesterday, today, and forever)* that will bring us into the Fullness of the knowledge of His Love, for only this can do it.

LOOK AT CHRIST IN EVERY AGE

When we study Prophecy, we are, in actual fact, looking at Christ in every Age, either as Prophet, Priest, or King. All too often we baulk at studying Prophecy, but this only comes about from 'strong delusion'. However, the world would not be deluded by Satan's devices (2 Corinthians 2:11) if it would give heed to the *'more sure Word of Prophecy'* (2 Peter 1:19) which reveals Satan's origins, purposes, and doom. But the Spirit of Prophecy is not only neglected, but also *discouraged* because of the way Scriptures are *'wrested'* (2 Peter 3:16).

Thus 'we have a very uncertain word of prophecy, to which you would do well to pay no attention whatsoever!' At this point, I can only ask if we are going to surrender to Satan so lightly? If you are a Christian, then your focus, and your direction, should be the *'Living Word of Christ'* in ALL its Glory (Psalm 111:2), and looking for Him to return and take us up. Not only that, but we are required to go out to the highways and byways and invite the good and the bad into the Marriage of the Lamb. (Matthew 22:9–10)

Let us now again clarify what prophecy really is so that there is no more confusion or delusion in this. In Revelation 19:10 it spells out what Prophecy is: *'for the testimony of Jesus is the Spirit of Prophecy.'* Now what can be clearer than that? Prophecy is not 'foretelling the future'; prophecy is not 'unfolding the past'; prophecy is not 'seeing what is happening elsewhere, or in men's hearts.' Without Christ in the picture, it is NOT Prophecy, only predictions, history, or even assumptions, for only Prophecy *(The Testimony of Jesus)* is listed as a SURE WORD. Yes, prophecy includes all of these things, but they are never enough on their own. Let's look at that verse in the Living Word of God:

> *We have also a MORE SURE word of prophecy;* ***whereunto ye do well to take heed****, as unto a light that shineth in a dark place, until the day dawn, and the daystar arise in your hearts; knowing this first, that no prophecy is of any private interpretation. For the prophecy came not in old time by the will of man:*

What is Prophecy?

but holy men spake as they were moved by the Holy Ghost.

2 Peter 1:19–21

(Emphases mine)

Of course, we may ask as to what these holy men were moved to speak, and the answer is, as I previously explained:

The Testimony of Our Lord and Saviour; Jesus Christ in ALL its Completeness, and Glory. Prophecy is clearly and finally about the **elucidation of God's Will and His Holy Word!**

All too often, they are presented to us in what is called 'Mystery' form, for:

> *'but the natural man receiveth not the things of the Spirit of God: for they are foolishness unto him: neither can he know them, because they are Spiritually discerned.'*

1 Corinthians 2:14

Yet, in verse 16, we are given the way to understand:

'for who hath known the mind of the Lord, that he may instruct Him? **But we have the mind of Christ.**'

This means that when we give the Testimony of Christ, He reveals His Mysteries to us, and nine of these are listed for us. These are as follows:

Mystery of the Gospel:	Ephesians 6:19
Mystery of Israel:	Romans 11:25
Mystery of Faith:	1 Timothy 3:9
Mystery of Godliness:	1 Timothy 3:16
Mystery of God's Will:	Ephesians 1:9
Mystery of the Wisdom of God:	1 Corinthians 2:7
Mystery of Iniquity:	2 Thessalonians 2:7
Mystery of Christ and the Church:	Ephesians 5:32
Mystery of Resurrection:	1 Corinthians 15:51

All of these are open to us for our understanding, if we just let God's Holy Spirit unravel them for us. Remember Proverbs 25:2.

We do not have to join Secret Societies or any other silly things like that, but only to PRAY for Wisdom and Understanding from the One True God, and it will be granted unto us. A Mystery is something that may be known when you have the

Keys to unlocking it, and Foundations to lay it on, and was NEVER meant to be completely unknown.

God has given us *all* the Keys to understanding His Word *right within His Word*, and we only need to use them, but never without His Holy Spirit to guide us. This book on prophecy is solely aimed at allowing you extra Keys, and Foundation Stones to use and build on, so that the things of God are not foolishness to you. By this, you may have the mind of Christ to testify of all these things, so that we may enter into His Rest for ALL Eternity, and that is why we teach you, and encourage you in these things, for the Lord has so called us to do this.

Within this, we should listen to that very same Word for instruction on how to behave, both towards our fellow members of mankind, and also to God. Church groups are teaching us wrong on too many occasions, and then they wonder why their attendance numbers are slipping. Our Lord Jesus Christ gave us the answer to our congregation numbers in Church in John chapter 12:

> ***And I, if I be lifted up from the earth, will draw all men unto Me.***
>
> John 12:32

There it is in a nutshell: the formula for numbers! If the Church groups acted more like we are asked to do in Holy Writ, then more people would see a Church worthy of attending, and actually go there. At least they would have an opportunity to make an informed choice, and have an opportunity to reject God for more truthful reasons than what we normally hear (right up until you start to asking them questions about what they really believe, and want. See also Psalm 53:1).

Many just want us to tolerate God, or reject Him, and yet, when you look (REALLY look) at what He has for us in His Creation for us (Romans 1:20), then we see so much more of why we should be on our hands and knees in front of Him. We need to stop being Pseudo-Christians (The *'good'* people of the world, and who have done more to harm the reputation of Christianity than anything else: *there is none good but the Father in Heaven*—Matthew 19:17), and get on with God's Business of Saving Souls. Also, if more 'Christians' were to know just what Christianity was, and wasn't, and acted accordingly, then the Unsaved would have a far greater chance of making the choice on real information, and I think that we would see a greater number in Church each week.

THE LAW OF OMISSION

So often we hear preachers and teachers sprouting their interpretations of what the Word of God is saying, and yet they leave out any and all passages that contradict their viewpoint. It is so much easier to push an agenda if you only give information that supports your case, and leave the rest out. It is the same with prophecy. Unless your teaching aligns with ALL of Scripture (100%), then it is questionable, and quite often, the prophetic teaching (thus also the prophecy) must be unfulfilled.

The Sabbath Day Advocates leave out anything to do with the 8th day (Sunday); the Sunday Worshippers leave out so much on the Sabbath, and so on. IT IS NOT A CASE OF EITHER/OR, BUT **BOTH**. The students of Prophecy leave out anything that does not align with their views on where it is headed and what it means, and so on. This is the Law of Omission, where you can alter an outcome by leaving out relevant details, and this is so common everywhere. Surely, the only way some ideas can gain any credibility, is to leave out the difficult bits, or even the impossible bits that clearly show that they are wrong somewhere.

Look, anytime that you hear that the Bible is 30% prophecy, or a quarter Prophetic, (instead of 100%), or any of these claims, then you can rightfully be assured that they are generally leaving important details out, so that they can justify a particular viewpoint that is not necessarily Biblical. Even the Red-Letter Bibles are guilty of this in some ways for, to many, ONLY the words in red are of any importance, and all else is of lesser value. This is so wrong! Every time you see a movie showing someone portraying Jesus, it will leave an impression on people of just what Jesus was like, and they ALL come up very short—giving a misguided idea about what Jesus the Christ was really like. The really important bits about Jesus's ability and bearing about being the actual Son of God are omitted, for no ordinary man can do that. The list goes on and is quite extensive, but it is not surmountable, for we can go into Holy Scripture—ALL of it—and get the correct information in ALL of its Glory and Truth. ONLY by checking, contrasting, and comparing ALL of Scripture can we tell if something is fully completed or not.

I hope that this gives you a better understanding of this aspect of our studies, so that you may go forth in your preparations for His Second Coming, knowing that His Word is sure!

It makes an Eternity of difference, and is for US!

AMEN

2
WHAT IS A CHRISTIAN?

As this is a book on Prophecy, you may well wonder why I have included this topic here. It is my personal belief that it is vital to have a REAL, RIGHT, AND REVERENT RELATIONSHIP with The Lord and Saviour, before you can receive a REAL, WISE, CLEAR, AND DISCERNING UNDERSTANDING of Bible Prophecy. This then entails knowing what the REAL, RIGHT, AND REVERENT RELATIONSHIP is. That makes it a very necessary foundational cornerstone, on which God can build His Church, and a key cornerstone in understanding Prophecy. Also, let us not forget that The Lord Himself is the 'Chief Cornerstone'; The 'Rock of Ages' on which we build our church.

How Do I know If I am A Christian?

I kept getting asked this question, *What is a Christian?*, so, here is a copy of a sermon I originally did on this subject back in 1997.

I'll start with a quote from a book *In The Twinkling Of An Eye* by Sydney Watson written in 1910. Abraham Cohen, a Jew, was speaking to Tom Hammond, a reporter, who had come to see him.

'He asked, "Are you a Christian, sir?" For a moment Tom Hammond was startled by the suddenness, the definiteness, of the question. He found no immediate word of reply. "You are a Gentile, of course, Mr. Hammond," the Jew went on; "but are you a Christian? For it is a curious fact that I find very few Gentiles whom I have met, even professed Christians, and fewer still who ever pretended to live up to their profession."

'Tom Hammond recovered himself sufficiently to say: "Yes, I am a Gentile, of course, and I suppose I am—er—" It struck him, as he floundered in the second half of his reply, as being very extraordinary that he should find it difficult to

What is Prophecy?

state why he supposed he was a Christian.

'While he hesitated, the Jew went on: "Why should you suppose, Sir? Is there nothing distinctive enough about the possession of Christianity to give assurance of it to its possessor? I do not suppose I am a Jew (by religion, I mean, and not merely by race). No Sir, I do not suppose, for I know it."'

I have heard a lot of people tell us how Christians are supposed to act, and what we should be doing for them, but, when you consider how <u>little</u> those same people know about Christianity, then I have to ask, why are we using them as the guidelines for this, especially with the bad press that goes along with it? So let us look at some of these *'aspects'* of Christianity, and other systems, to see if there is a difference.

The first thing that people say is **Believing in God.** However, the first thing that must be asked here is: *'Who or What do you refer to as God?'*

Even if it is The One True God you believe in, then that would only make you a follower of the Jewish faith, and not a Christian, but nonetheless Christians do believe in The One True God.

Prayer. Christians pray—so, does praying make you a Christian? Of course, the answer is NO, it does not. Many religions include prayer in their beliefs systems and ordinances. The Buddhists even have prayer wheels that you spin, and the prayer written on the wheel goes out every time the wheel turns. Prayer does not make us Christian, but prayer *is* a part of Christianity.

Let us look at **Going to Church**, or other place of worship. Again, the only answer is that this does not make us Christian, any more than the other religions going to their Temples or on pilgrimages. However, going to Church *is* a part of being a Christian, but does not involve a specific church or building of man.

How about having **a Holy Book**? No, many of the other systems also have their Holy Books, and reading these will not make you a Christian. However, reading our Holy Bible *is* part of Christianity.

Being **Religious**! Surely that is it. However, when you ask people what they mean when they refer to someone as being 'religious', they say, *'You know—Christianity.'* Are they saying that no-one else is religious, or that other religions are not religions at all? We know that that is not true, so, what are they really saying? It all stems from a very poor understanding of what constitutes a 'Religion'. To be *'religious'* actually means to have *'a standard of Morals, Principles, Ethics, and Code of Conduct; a system of beliefs.'*

ALL belief systems and *every person alive*, including the Atheists, Humanists, and Secularists, have such a system in some form or another. (Actually, when someone says that they are not religious at all, they are publicly stating that they have NO Morals, Principles, Ethics, or Standards to live by, and I am not so sure I would want to be around anyone like that). Even worse is when they focus on 'the form' over 'what is believed', which is Religiosity, not religion! So, just being 'Religious' does not make us Christians at all, but being a Christian does mean that we are to have these things as our standards, especially as ours were given to us by God Himself, and all the others came up with their own version of that.

What about **Obeying the Laws and Commandments**? Will that make us Christian? The answer is NO! At best it will make you a follower of Judaism, but even this is not guaranteed. Other religious systems also have their Laws and Commandments and they are expected to obey them just as much as we are, and so, this is not the criteria to become a Christian, but *Obeying God and His Laws **is*** part of being Christian.

Speaking about the Laws and Commandments, have you noticed that, originally our Laws of this, our Land, are based on Judeo-Christian teachings? These Principles are what we built our societies on, and they allowed us to walk down the street at night unmolested. They allowed us to feel safe in our homes, but the world is trying to get rid of them, even though most other religions now have our principles overlaid on them. (It was the Christians that allowed women to vote, to drive, to go to school, and so on, but these things do not make us Christian either). So, does just following the Local laws make you a Christian? No, it doesn't.

Our Constitutions in America and Australia, the Magna Carta, and so on, have great foundations, for they are based on Judeo-Christian teachings, but does **following our Constitutions** make us Christian? No, Christians are told to give to

Caesar what is Caesar's, but we are also to follow God, through Jesus Christ, and by the power of the Holy Spirit.

Being Tolerant makes a good Christian—yes? No! We are not to tolerate Sin being done to us, or by us. These tolerance teachings of today go against what we are taught to do by Christ, when we are told not to tolerate them, but to *rebuke sin* and the devil's ways. We are to differentiate (discern/discriminate) between 'exclusive' and 'inclusive' teachings; from what is right and what is wrong.

Loving everybody and everything! Surely that is the answer, but, NO, it isn't. Christians are not to love Sin, either by us, or by others. We are to treat others *with* Love, and bring them out of their Fallen State *through* God's Word, and by the Outcome of what Jesus of Nazareth did for us on the Cross, and that is to *'die for us while we were yet sinful'* to Redeem us back to God, and lovingly share that message with them. So, loving everyone and everything is not what makes us Christian. However, Christians love others because G*od first loved us.*

Doing Good Deeds! Surely that makes us Christians—and the answer can only be NO! There are a lot of religious systems that encourage good deeds, for all sorts of reasons, but just doing good deeds does not make us Christian. In fact, the do-gooders of the world have done more to discredit Christianity than anyone else ever has, especially when you ask them for any definition of 'What is Good?'. We need to STOP being Pseudo-Christians (The *'good'* people of the world, since *there is none good but the Father in Heaven:* Matthew 19:17), and get on with God's Business of Saving Souls. As Christians, we *are* expected to do good deeds, but not to *make* us Christian, but because God gives to us freely, and it is up to us to share that goodness with those around us. None of us can buy our way into heaven by doing deeds! Not all religions share their goodness and blessings with those in need, even of their own systems. What does that say about their religions that they do not even help their own? (At least our God gave us clear definitions of what is good and what is wrong, AND why we should listen to, and act on that!) Discernment is needed here. *Works* goes against *Grace*, and none of us can **earn** our way into Heaven—none of us can appease God for our sins by good works alone.

> *Not by works of righteousness which we have done, but according to His mercy He saved us, by the washing of regeneration, and renewing of the Holy Ghost.*
>
> Titus 3:5

How about a specific good deed, like **Tithing** to the Church? Again, the answer can only be NO! People all over the world give to their religions in all sorts of ways—right from things and monies, all the way up to giving their very lives for them. No, Tithing is not just a Christian thing to do, nor does tithing make us Christian. However, we are not to forget to Tithe, as it is told as something for us to do, by God Himself.

In the list above, we see a thing called **Discernment**, so does being discerning make us into Christians? No, sadly, it doesn't! Other religions call for discernment also of their beliefs, and who is utilising them. Discernment is used by those who are part of these, but discernment does not make any of them into Christians. Once we know what God wants for us to do, then it is up to us to discern if we are doing it, but that is its limit.

Is it **Calling on Jesus**? Is that what makes us Christian? Well, only sort of, for Jesus was a common name back in the first century, and I even worked with a gentleman whose name was Jesus Barnabas. If I was only calling out to Jesus, without identifying just which Jesus, then I might be calling to him to come and save my soul, and *he* couldn't even save himself.

Being '**Born-Again**'. Yes, we have heard that *this* is the defining quantity, and yet, when you look at it, then it is not. You will be amazed at just how many races and cultures believe in the dying to the old self, and being rebirthed and reborn, even as part of their rituals of adulthood. Even the Occultists have this belief, through the process of Alchemy, and I definitely CANNOT say that these are Christians. However, being born-again is a part of Christianity, for sure.

I could include things like **Fellowship, Baptism, Repentance,** and a whole host of others, with a similar lack of success.

What is Prophecy?

OK. We are starting to run out of individual things to list, and none of these make us a Christian. Hang on, **what about a combination of them?** Let us put together 'good deeds' and 'prayer'. No, that doesn't work. How about 'believing in God' and 'going to Church'? No good there either, as that still does not make us a Christian! How about 'going to church' and 'prayer'; no, that didn't work either. I know, let us put more of them together, say, like 'prayer', 'church', and 'good deeds'. Still no good, for even these together do not give any guarantee of being a Christian. Even if we put **all of them together**, we will always come up short. So, what are we to do? Where do we go to find the answers?

Fortunately, we can find the answers to this, and it is listed IN our Holy Book, which we call the *Bible*. In this, we are told to Gather Together in Worship and Praise, to Pray, to Obey the Laws and Commandments, and all the other things we have mentioned here together, but there is a DIFFERENCE to the other religions, and that is our RELATIONSHIP WITH GOD (*not* Religiosity), and the set of directions to establish that. Christianity is the *only* Religion that extolls Humility; all others extol might, strength, wealth, and power.

The Humility of God is truly something to consider. God, who deserves *everything* that we can bring to Him in Praise and Worship, gives the Glory to His Son, whom we call Our Lord Jesus Christ. Our Lord Jesus Christ is so Humble that He says it is of His Father in Heaven, and then gives it over to God's Holy Spirit, leaving the Holy Spirit to have the Glory that is due from giving His very Life for our Salvation. The Holy Spirit states that it is of God, and thus He is the one who is worthy, and that Our Lord and Saviour is the one who did it for us. NONE OF THEM WANT THE SPOTLIGHT for the Glory! Each one is willing to give this glory to the others, and then they go and pass it all over to us humans who are Redeemed by this Wonderful Grace. Such Humility is completely different to how we humans act: a 180-degree turnaround (we act in completely the opposite direction and manner to this). Such Humility is refreshing to watch, and worth entering into.

One more thing about their Humility, and that is where they want US to share in it as well! THEY DON'T JUST WANT US TO SEE IT, BUT TO BE PART OF

IT. Have you considered just how Humble you have to be to want to share so much of everything, without cost? And so maybe now you should.

Judaism and Christianity are somewhat different to the other religions, for in the other religions, man is seeking God, or to be gods themselves, but here, GOD IS SEEKING MAN. Not only is He seeking Man, but ***He gives the directions on how to get back to Him***, for us to be all together for Eternity, and ***then He makes it possible by giving His only Son to die for us***, so that the necessary Blood Price is paid in full. Because of this Great Act of Love by the Creator for us, then a way has been given to us, and that Way is clearly outlined for us.

> *Jesus saith unto him, I am the way, the truth, and the life: no man cometh unto the Father, but by Me.*
>
> John 14:6

Notice that this is an *exclusive* statement (NO MAN *cometh unto the Father, but by Me*), and not inclusive like those 'tolerance' and 'love everything' teachings. See also the Book of 1 Peter.

Even then, it is up to us to *discern* just which specific Jesus we are dealing with—and it is Our Lord Jesus Christ, the only Son of God, who came to us as Jesus of Nazareth, by a virgin birth, in Bethlehem, died for us on a cross of wood, and so on, clearly defining just which Jesus. This discernment we need is only done properly when it is from the Holy Spirit who teaches us in all things, and is sent from the Father in Heaven, whom is God. (1 Corinthians 12:3; 1 John 2:27)

ONLY by having *this* Jesus as the centre of our Worship, with our focus on God, and being led by His Holy Spirit, looking forward to His (Our Lord Jesus Christ's) coming again, will we ever be good Christians. Christ MUST be the centre of *Christ*-ianity! THIS IS THE ONLY DEFINITION THAT MAKES ANY SENSE, and is the only one which fits *all* the criteria.

Some say this is a problem, for this then raises a question, for they ask if this God *forces* Himself on us to *make* us Christian. This can easily be answered, for none of these things will *make* us a Christian, it is something which we **choose** to be, NOT forced to be, and even then, it is usually after we realise just who God is and how BIG our need for Him in our lives is.

God will not violate the threshold of the kingdom of man's spirit. He will only enter when He is invited to do so. The wages of sin is death, but the gift of God is eternal life through Jesus Christ our Lord. THIS is where we find that *Peace of God* that lies outside man's understanding. We either accept, or reject this wonderful gift by our will, and take this decision into eternity.

Only AFTER we *give ourselves over to God*, through Our Lord Jesus Christ, and by the power of the Holy Spirit, do we do the rest of this list AS Christians. Christianity is defined by what THE Christ did for us, and we do good deeds as a result. We pray as a result of this; we go to Church as a result; we love others as a result of this, and so on for all of it. In short, we are known by our Fruit, but the first and foremost fruit is the Love of: God, Our Lord Jesus Christ, and God's Holy Spirit.

Wade Robinson said:

'Today, Christ is chiefly known by the opposition He provokes, and the hatred that is levelled against Him.' Sadly, this is true of Christianity as

well, but it need not be the case, especially if we were more to conduct ourselves as 'Christian' to those around us.

It is time for us to re-examine our Christianity to see if we ARE really acting out our part, according to this definition. Let us not 'suppose' we are Christians, let us be SURE OF IT to all around us, and be ready to answer, both in season and out of season, as to WHY we are like this, and WHY we choose it.

Also, **if more 'Christians' were to know just what Christianity was, and wasn't, and acted accordingly, then the Unsaved would have a far greater chance of making the choice on real information, and I think that we would see a greater number in Church each week.** END-OF-STORY!

When you do get into God's Word, or possibly even a church group, then please don't expect God to act like your footstool, your butler, or even a vending machine where you put in a cheap prayer and every desire of your heart automatically comes out the chute: it won't do you any good, for God is none of these things. Don't try to barter

What is Prophecy?

with Him about what you might do. Instead, take a good long hard look at just Who and what He is, and act accordingly, both in prayer as well as in your study of Him. This means that, no matter how much you think you are getting it right, being good, righteous, and worthy, then God may be seeing it a bit differently from *His* perspective, which is different from yours.

You are being tested unto Righteousness, as are all mankind, and the prize is God's Love that has also been put to the test, and proved Faithful, all the way to Salvation on a Cross, and well beyond into Eternity.

Are you someone who comes *to* Church, or are you *part of* God's Church?

I cannot exhort you enough to not despise Prophecy, for it is the key to Wisdom and Understanding, and Eternal Life. It is the Key to unlocking what God would have us do, and how we are to do it. It is the foundation that we stand on!

Amen

GOD-BOTHERERS

Naturally, the questions and comments, even accusations, did not stop there, and so I need to clarify even more. (Some people are really against any talk of prophecy). I would like to address another thing that Christians get accused of on a semi-regular basis, and that is being *'God-Botherers.'*

While it is yet another topic, I decided to put it here for convenience, as it IS a comment that requires addressing. The word usage is interesting, and needs to be assessed.

Christians are often referred to as *'God-Botherers'* by many secular people, and is clearly meant to be a put-down to us (just like the word 'Christian' often is). Even our time in Fellowship and Worship is referred to as *'God-Bothering',* and so it is time to address this, for we need to know what is being spoken of here, and ask if it does relate to us at all.

When you look at a dictionary, you see that *'bother'* is referred to as a negative word: *Pester, worry, be troublesome,* and *trouble.*

Not once did I see it listed as a positive, and that would be a mistake, for there are positive usages of the word, like bothering to take time to help; bothering to love our God, spouse, children, and so on. These are clearly positives! None of our relationships would work without someone taking the time to bother; none of us would ever receive assistance if nobody bothered to answer our calls for help, etcetera. Imagine what the world would be like if no-one bothered to do these things.

However, there ARE negative aspects, and it is obvious that these connotations are what is being meant when we are accused of being *'botherers'*. Let us look at whether or not we deserve this title.

The first question is this: ***Are we bothering God as people—being God Botherers?***

To answer that, we must find out what God would be bothered by, and to answer that, we need to get into His Word on the subject. Here we see that God is DELIGHTED in those who come to Him, and He is offended when we rebuke Him. So, *it is those who rebuke God and His Son Jesus, even those that reject His Holy Spirit who are really bothering Him.*

God is clearly not bothered by those who work WITH Him, but only by those who oppose Him.

Yes, God does bother to give us His Love, His Mercy, His Grace, His Son to die for us so that we may return to Him as His Own, and so much more, but God loves to do this, and these are not negatives to Him. However, He is troubled/bothered when we reject His free Gifts for us; He worries about us when we choose death over Eternal Life; He pesters us to come to Him, but we refuse, and so on, which makes those others the REAL God-Botherers, and He caters to that.

The second question would be: ***Do we bother God as a Church?***

God established the Church through His Son, Our Lord Jesus the Christ, by the Power of the Holy Spirit, and it is a pleasure to Him that we become part of His Church. Yes, *He does get bothered by those who distort His Church and His teachings that He established through His Son, the Holy Word,* but not with those who want to get it right and just BELIEVE and OBEY. We see many Bible Passages that warn and tell us of this. God bothered to give us His Word and His Prophets to show us the Way back to Him as part of His Church. He bothered to give us Creation so that we had a place to live, and the opportunity to live

What is Prophecy?

there for all Eternity as part of that Church, and He did this willingly, not as a drain on Himself, but for the Glory to be shared with us all, if only we accept it. It is those who refuse such wonderful Gifts that are a worry and bother to Him, for it grieves Him to see many go astray and miss out as a result.

Every question we can come up with comes to the same conclusion: Those who want to be with God and are doing something about it, are a Pleasure to God, while *those who do not want to accept the wonderful Salvation and resultant Heaven, are a* bother (negative usage of the word) to God, *so, just who are the God-botherers?* **It can only be those same Secularists and people who accuse us of it!** As always, it is the Devil and his adherents who accuse and blame others of their own crimes. Again, God is clearly not bothered by those who work with Him, but He *is* bothered by those who go against Him.

So, if you do not wish to be a 'God-Botherer', then get in accordance with the Will of God, and work with Him.

Be not confounded and deceived by anything else, nor give into False Accusation, for that is of the enemy: The Devil!

INSTEAD: SERVE GOD!

3

THE END OF PROPHECY

Can a book as ancient as the Bible really be relevant today? Can it shed light on Modern challenges? Many consider that it is an outdated model of stories, moral teachings, and laws of little relevance to today. This type of thinking pushes the Bible back into the distant past, with no escape possible. By classifying the Bible as ancient history, it then gives room for us to ignore what is contained within, and replace them with more popular philosophies of our modern times, more in line with what *we* would want for ourselves. Some say, *'God has left us,'* and *'God does not see us!'* (Ezekiel 8:12)

This type of argument is often referred to as the 'Immanence — Eminence' equation: whether God is out there only, waiting for a time to return, if at all, **or**, up close and personal at every moment of every day. The 'out there only' schools of thought (like some denominations of so-called Christianity) are all rooted in Platonic Philosophies, where, if there is any god, he/she/it can only be at a distance from mankind. This is in stark contrast to the Judeo-Christian God who IS out there for sure, looking upon us and all that we do, but ALSO up close and personal to each and every one of us, on a moment-by-moment basis.

There is also the school of thought that God is so close to us, that there is nothing that happens without him causing it. This is also in disagreement with what we know about God, for He is not the author of evil for us. That title belongs to another.

Israel has been given many prophets over time, and only some of them have been recorded for us. In line with Jewish thinking, it is only those who were recognised as having a message for future generations that were written down. This is also true of the Narrative Books, like Joshua, Judges, Samuel, and Kings. Deborah, Ruth, Samson,

What is Prophecy?

Hannah, Samuel, Esther, and David, all provide wonderful insights to our own mistakes, and give incredible outlines to how we should be living. Every book thus recorded was seen to serve as a guidebook for all future generations of the Jews. In other words, we, as Christians, do not study the Bible to learn about the history of the Jews, but to glean guidance for ourselves as we stumble along the very same paths in life that they encountered. We're just as much a part of fallen mankind as they are. Their mistakes are exactly the same as ours, even today, and so it is relevant to us today in our own walk with God. Also, if we look at Deuteronomy:

> *O that there were such an heart in them, that they would fear me, and keep all my commandments always, that it might be well with them,* ***and with their children for ever!***
>
> Deuteronomy 5:29

In this, we see that God's Words will cover us forever. What God has included in His Word for us will also continue forever, or as long as is needed, which includes our modern times.

> *For verily I say unto you, Till heaven and earth pass, one jot or one tittle **shall in no wise pass** from the law, till all be fulfilled.*
>
> Matthew 5:18
>
> *Jesus Christ the same yesterday, and to day, **and for ever**.*
>
> Hebrews 13:8

The more we adopt the approach of listening to God and what He has to say for us, including in the writings of the Prophets, the more we can come into alignment to His Word and Will for us today. Thus, if we adopt the approach of *absorbing the meaning* of the Word of God, by the power given to us through The Holy Spirit of God, then **we will better understand our position in the events of our time**. God cannot bring it out of us, if we never put it in first. It will also lead us into a better understanding of the Process of Redemption; that we are living in the *'Beginnings'* of our own redemption, and then to act in the necessary first steps to speeding its arrival! Yes, when the Books of the Prophets were written, our Redemption was still a very future event, and even Daniel was told to:

> *But thou, O Daniel,* **shut up the words**, *and* SEAL THE BOOK, ***even to the time of the end:*** *many shall run to and fro, and knowledge shall be increased.*
>
> Daniel 12:4

This shows that it was not to be revealed until the 'Time of The End', and then it was to be opened up to the people, for only then would they appreciate what was written within—and be able to act on it! That alone makes it very relevant to us today as we approach the End Times ourselves! (Now, I want you to go to the Book of Revelation, and you will see that John is NOT told to seal up this work! This is important in our understanding). We are so much closer to the final day than ever before, and so we ARE to study and consider prayerfully what is contained within—ALL of it. However, it also implies a time when these things will all be 'Past-Tense", and no longer needed as a roadmap for us to follow.

To answer this, we must go to Revelation and to 1 Corinthians 13:

> *But in the days of the voice of the seventh angel, when he shall begin to sound, **the mystery of God should be finished, as He hath declared to His servants** THE PROPHETS.*
>
> Revelation 10:7

> *Charity never faileth: but whether there be prophecies, they shall fail; whether there be tongues, they shall cease; whether there be knowledge, it shall vanish away. For we know in part, and we prophesy in part. **But when that which is** PERFECT **is come, then that which is in part shall be done away**. When I was a child, I spake as a child, I understood as a child, I thought as a child: but when I became a man, I put away childish things. For now we see through a glass, darkly; but then face to face: now I know in part; but then shall I know even as also I am known.*
>
> 1 Corinthians 13:8–12

Firstly, we need to focus on the word τέλειος ('teleios'), which is used in verse 10, and translated as *perfect* ('that which is perfect'), but also means *wanting nothing necessary to completeness*—similar in meaning to our word, *holy*.

God's Word is as Complete as God's Will:

> *And the word which ye hear is not Mine, but the Father's which sent Me.*
>
> John 14:24

As He is Perfect/Holy, He has no need of change to get His message through. If He needed to make changes constantly, then what was chosen to do was not perfect in the first place. Fortunately, we do not have to worry about that, for it is sure. God's Word is complete, and we see this in passages like 2 John 1:5–9, where we are NOT writing new Commandments but:

> *This is the commandment, that, as ye have heard from the beginning, ye should walk in it.*
>
> 2 John 1:6

In verse 12 of 1 Corinthians 13, we get the idea, for we start out seeing through a glass darkly, but then we have prophecy, where God's Will is clarified and testified, so that we now see and know more fully. When you look at all this, then it is no wonder that Paul would want all of us to prophesy as he states in 1 Corinthians 14:1 and 3:

> *Follow after charity, and desire spiritual gifts, but **rather that ye may prophesy**.*
>
> 1 Corinthians 14:1

> *But **he that prophesieth speaketh unto men to edification, and exhortation, and comfort**.*
>
> 1 Corinthians 14:3

However, what is clear is that God is NOT doing anything new outside of His Written Word! What is written is PERFECT and therefore needs no alterations! He is doing the same old things, only to new people, and *that* is where many false ideas of God doing new things comes from. The rest come from our false knowledge where we think we know more than God on most subjects, but that is folly—Jeremiah 51:17,18; Romans 10:2; Proverbs 3:7; 1 Corinthians 8:1; and Ephesians 3:19.

It also means a time when we will no longer need these things, for we will know as He wants us to know, for we will put away the childish things that were required for us to understand while we were looking through that dark glass. Tongues are not required when we speak the same language; healing will be done via the leaves of the Tree of Life (Revelation 22:2) and not via things we would wish for in our false knowledge; there will be no need to proclaim the Glory of God to others by way of tongues, as we will all be right there in the middle of it. Also notice the word *'nations'* is used for when the leaves are to be used for healing. Does this mean that there will still be areas of different language groups, meaning the gift of tongues will still be needed? Look again at 1 Corinthians 13:

> *Charity never faileth: but whether there be prophecies, they shall fail; whether there be tongues,* **they shall cease;** *whether there be knowledge, it shall vanish away.*
>
> 1 Corinthians 13:8

The word *cease* is 'pauo', which means *to come to a complete stop*. Also the gift of knowledge (special knowledge of unrevealed truth) shall *vanish away*, for we will all be with God in His Kingdom as part of His Great Family; knowing all that He wants us to know. In short, we will become part of God's Family, living in His Glory, doing things the way He always meant us to be doing, and I do believe that that is something to accept as part of our Choices in Life. While we are on the subject of tongues and prophecy, I want to point out the clear difference between these gifts:

> *Wherefore tongues are for a sign, not to them that believe, but to them that believe not: but prophesying serveth not for them that believe not, but for them which believe.*
>
> 1 Corinthians 14:22

In Daniel chapter 9, we are given a timeline on prophecy being sealed up, but even that needs to be placed into correct context.

> *Seventy weeks are determined upon thy people and upon thy holy city, to finish the transgression, and to make an end of sins, and to make reconciliation for iniquity, and to bring in everlasting righteousness, and to* **seal up the vision and prophecy,** *and to anoint the most Holy.*
>
> Daniel 9:24

What is Prophecy?

Here we are talking about the Lord and Saviour fulfilling the prophecies about the REDEMPTION OF ALL MANKIND GIVEN THROUGH SHED BLOOD, and this vision of God about redeeming us, is now correctly sealed for all time through what was done for us on a cross of wood by His Son: Our Saviour. This timeline was correctly completed *exactly* as told to us in Daniel. However, our Salvation was not finalised then, for we still had to know the difference in how we approach God and His Mercies, and CHOOSE which one we would exercise in our own lives. This is the litmus test of whether we see clearly, or not. This is further exemplified in the story of Creation, where we were to be given time according to God's Calendar of events, to come to the seventh day, and then the eighth; to and through the 1,000 years of Rest, and then on to Eternity.

Let us continue on our discussion regarding the 'end' of prophecy.

Paul, in his address to the mature Church in Ephesians 4:11, speaks of individual giftings such as apostles and prophets. Wuest notes that *apostles* is used in the 'secondary sense' of 'those who proclaim the word of God today'; prophets, 'refers not to those who foretell the future, but to preachers and expounders of the word.' (Wuest's comments on Ephesians 4:11–12).

> *And He gave some, apostles; and some, prophets; and some, evangelists; and some, pastors and teachers; For the perfecting of the saints, for the work of the ministry, for the edifying of the body of Christ.*
>
> Ephesians 4:11–12

Prophecy is 'clarifying God's Word for His purposes…' and the prophet's role as the 'elucidation of God's Word and His Will,' but collectively his role as part of a wider ministry is for *'the perfecting* (maturing) *of the saints, for the work of the ministry, for the edifying of the body of Christ.* This until we all come in the unity of the faith, and of the knowledge of the Son of God, unto a perfect (mature) man, unto the measure of the fullness of Christ':

> [11] *And He gave some, apostles; and some, prophets; and some, evangelists; and some, pastors and teachers;* [12] *For the perfecting of the saints, for the work of the*

ministry, for the edifying of the body of Christ: ¹³ *Till we all come in the unity of the faith, and of the knowledge of the Son of God, unto a perfect man, unto the measure of the stature of the fulness of Christ:* ¹⁴ *That we henceforth be no more children, tossed to and fro, and carried about with every wind of doctrine, by the sleight of men, and cunning craftiness, whereby they lie in wait to deceive;* ¹⁵ *But speaking the truth in love, may grow up into Him in all things, which is the head, even Christ:* ¹⁶ *From whom the whole body fitly joined together and compacted by that which every joint supplieth, according to the effectual working in the measure of every part, maketh increase of the body unto the edifying of itself in love.*

Ephesians 4:11–16

The 'work of the ministry', in a nutshell, is speaking the truth in love 'to build up the Church (including the process of the demolishing of any false doctrines) and to bring in lost souls to The Kingdom of God.'

This infers that Prophecy is no longer just a Gift, but a ministry of exposition and illumination, but it is still required to be a Gift from God to conduct this ministry properly. We are also to notice that Paul's list goes on from prophets, to evangelists, and then lists pastors and teachers. This means that the teachers are not all prophets, but all prophets are teachers in some form. The prophet is thus one who rightly divides the Word of God, thereby making it necessary for him to be up on his exegesis, not only from his position of correct interpretation from the Holy Spirit of God, but also on the other erroneous frameworks, so that he can correctly and effectively rebut them (hence the need for knowledge and wisdom to be a part of the ministry of the Prophet).

Much prayer for Wisdom and Understanding is clearly involved to reach this point, not to mention an interaction with God's Holy Spirit. This before you share, or teach, or your foundations are not on The Rock of Ages, but on sand. The listener/student needs to know exactly where you stand on any given topic regarding God, or they can, and will, insert their own concepts and presuppositions into the mix.

What is Prophecy?

C.S. Lewis compared teaching to shepherding sheep along a pathway. *'If you leave any gates open along the way, they will wander off into these instead of where you need them to be led.'* As I have worked with sheep on stations, I can testify that this is very true. We need to keep bringing the sheep back towards the destination, instead of wandering off to be eaten by wolves and other predators. Even to administer animal husbandry to maintain their health, or tend them in some other way, we need to get them to where we need them to be.

Every person needs a prophet like this; every Church needs a prophet like this, but that does not mean that every church building or group should have such a prophet *within their congregation*. No! Paul conducted such a role for many churches in the New Testament, and ministered and conveyed to them by means of his epistles to them, which carried the messages of edification, exhortation, and correction within his words for them.

Let us now go back to 1 Corinthians, chapter 13, and look at a few more of the words used, so that we may gain a greater understanding of what we are being told.

> *Charity never **faileth**: but whether there be prophecies, they shall fail; whether there be tongues, they shall cease; whether there be knowledge, it shall **vanish** (fail) away.*
>
> 1 Corinthians 13:8

FAILETH: 'ekpipto', *to drop away.* Love is permanent and 'shall never drop away.'

FAIL: 'katargeo', *to render entirely unnecessary,* also, *abolish, cease, destroy, do away, become of no effect, come to nought, put away (down), vanish away, make void.* Prophecy had its place in the period before the completion of the Bible; its function was to provide new revelation, along with correctly interpreting what was already given. But, when the Scriptures were complete (the correct translation of *'perfect'* in 1 Corinthians 13:10), the gift of providing 'new' revelation would be 'rendered entirely unnecessary.' The Holy Spirit illuminates the prophetic word, but He is no longer revealing new truths as He did by way of the gift when the Bible was incomplete. Since

What is Prophecy?

the completion that occurred within the Old and New Testaments that are already given to us by God, there is no need for 'added revelation'. We can know that this is sealed off, by seeing the 'end-cap' in Revelation 22:18–19.

This is an important aspect that we need to keep in mind today, where we see many 'prophets' giving *'new'* revelation that is not in our Holy Scriptures already, or even to remove something they do not agree with. Go to Revelation 22:

> *For I testify unto every man that heareth the words of the prophecy of this book, If any man shall add unto these things,* ***God shall add unto him the plagues that are written in this book:*** *And if any man shall take away from the words of the book of this prophecy,* ***God shall take away his part out of the book of life,*** *and out of the holy city, and from the things which are written in this book.*
>
> Revelation 22:18–19

This is certainly clear enough about adding *'new'* revelations to the Holy Scriptures, or removing something that we do not agree with, and thus definitely not something for us to do as a result. (The Word of God is complete, and Holy!) This is also part of the role of prophecy within the church, and the extra role is of 'correction'! We all need correction at times, especially when we are still learning about all that God has for us, and how He plans to get it to us, not to mention of our fallen nature in the meantime. The role of the Prophet is thus also to correct wrong, or 'new' teachings, that go outside of the Written Word of God.

We now need to go back to the beginning of this topic, where we have this:

> *But in the days of the voice of the seventh angel, when he shall begin to sound,* ***the mystery of God should be finished, as He hath declared to His servants*** *THE PROPHETS.*
>
> Revelation 10:7

The timing of this is clearly at the End of Days (the *seventh* angel), and just before the 1,000 years are established. That means that we are then about to witness the greatest event of the last couple of thousand years, but may well go right back to the beginning of time itself. **'The Mystery of God**

should be finished'—just as He has declared. Now there is a definite boundary on the need for a prophet to elucidate on the Word of God, and, to many, that is the ultimate range of the need for prophets to declare about God to the world in general. Prophecy has no need to go any further; that seems to be what it is saying!

However, I want you to think on something— when we read our Scriptures, then we will see that not everything will be fully complete at that time. There will be some who do not go up to the Mountain of The Lord during the millennium, meaning their rain will be cut off (Zechariah 14:17); Satan will be released after the 1,000 years leading to another time of war against God:

> ***And when the thousand years are expired, Satan shall be loosed out of his prison***, *And shall go out to deceive the nations which are in the four quarters of the earth, Gog and Magog, to gather them together to battle: the number of whom is as the sand of the sea. And they went up on the breadth of the earth, and compassed the camp of the saints about, and the beloved city: and fire came down*

> *from God out of heaven, and devoured them. And the devil that deceived them was cast into the lake of fire and brimstone, where the beast and the false prophet are, and shall be tormented day and night for ever and ever.*
>
> Revelation 20:7–10

When you take a closer look at these passages, you will see that it is not to be just the 1,000 years only, but that there will be an extension of the 1,000 years for Satan to deceive the nations and bring them to war against God (when the thousand years are expired—finished, THEN Satan is loosed—*shall be:* future tense). There is an extension of time given, and this for the purpose of people being able to see the difference, and so choose—just as happened with Noah and the Ark when the door was left open for another seven days. (Genesis 7:9–10) This is a very important detail that so many miss, for it is prophetic of how God is keeping the door open to so many of us right up to the very last minute!

Up until that time, however, God's people will still be taking messages and leaves for healing out to the people and nations, and so on. The

Mystery might be finished, but there appears to be a definite carry-over in the need for prophets to speak the Word of The Lord to them (an extension of time).

So, we must then ask this: 'Will we still have prophets right up to the time when the old earth and the old heavens are melted away to be replaced with the New Heaven and Earth, or do they disappear from the records during the millennium?' I will not give a definitive answer to this right now, but it is certainly something to think about.

> *[11] And I saw a great white throne, and Him that sat on it, from whose face the earth and the heaven fled away; and there was found no place for them. [12] And I saw the dead, small and great, stand before God; and the books were opened: and another book was opened, which is the book of life: and the dead were judged out of those things which were written in the books, according to their works. [13] And the sea gave up the dead which were in it; and death and hell delivered up the dead which were in them: and*

> *they were judged every man according to their works. ⁴¹And death and hell were cast into the lake of fire. This is the second death. ¹⁵ And whosoever was not found written in the book of life was cast into the lake of fire.*
>
> Revelation 20:11–15

At this point in time, we cannot guarantee absolutely that the other gifts will cease at the beginning of the millennium either, or at the time of the Second Resurrection, but we do know for certain that the need for them will completely disappear when we are all living in proper relationship with each other in God's Garden for us in Eternity. However, let us never forget that they WILL disappear when no longer required! This means that the other gifts are also included in the temporary files, which will be deleted when no longer needed. This then leads us to now investigate the temporary nature of the gifts, wonders, and miracles we see or read about now. Let us look at the timing and severity of such occurrences and see if there is a pattern.

SIGNS AND WONDERS

These subjects are clearly the source of so much dissension within the Churches, and there is no real need for that, except to demonstrate just how much influence Satan has within the walls of our churches. The Pentecostal Signs and Wonders has divided Christianity, and never so more than today. The Traditional Churches declare that they are all fakery and foolery, and the Pentecostal demonstrate various signs with great abandon at times (often to their detriment); wondering why the more traditional churches are NOT doing them. Which is correct? To answer this, we need to go back and see a bit of a timeline on their usages—a little history lesson.

Start out by reading the Creation Account in the Book of Genesis (read the first 3 chapters), and you will see God conducting some big-ticket items on the List of Signs. They seem to mostly drop out of sight up until the time we see God and Noah working together (however, it's worth taking note of Enoch in that interim), leading up to another big-ticket item: the Great Flood (Genesis 6:9–8:22), which happened because the people were departing from anything Godly. God needed to bring about a situation where the People of God could exist. So far, all the Signs and Wonders are being carried out by God, and not by mankind, except for a couple of instances, as with Enoch.

Then we see God's messengers—angels—visiting Abraham. At this point, we see God establishing a set group of people to work with, and through. (Let us never forget that God did not get caught out and so suddenly have to come up with Plan B. He already had everything covered, and was just executing His Plan as, and when required).

Next, we come to the Exodus where God starts to bring His Signs and Wonders to be used by His People, for the Israelite Nation was now being formed. Yes, He still had to do the big-ticket items Himself, like dividing the Red Sea; water from a rock; and miraculously feeding them, and so on. However He was now working closer with His People, and initially through Moses and Aaron (*two;* not just *one*, like with Enoch). These were 'birthing signs' for the young infant Nation; vehicles for their Faith and Belief to start—a foundation for their relationship with God. Signs, miracles, and wonders, keep cropping up along the way, but they are not the normal for most people. However, the means for them to continue at some time has been put in place, and that 'means' is the Israelite Nation. When you look at it, these were the 'milk' that was being fed to them, until they received the 'meat' on the mountain by way of Moses, and the Law/s received there. (First physically by way of the Manna, and then Spiritually by way of the Words of God).

Even before Moses took them on the Exodus, another miracle took place, and that was the burning bush that Moses saw. We can only assume how long that the bush had been burning before someone like Moses noticed. How many others had walked right on by that very bush, just because they did not 'see' God at work around them? I wonder how many times Moses had walked by it before he noticed? I wonder if you can see the close relationship to what we are being told in 1 Corinthians 13:12?

> *[11] When I was a child, I spake as a child, I understood as a child, I thought as a child: but when I became a man, I put away childish things. [12] For now we see through a glass, darkly; but then face to*

> *face: now I know in part; but then shall I know even as also I am known.*
>
> 1 Corinthians 13:11–12

Just like us today, they were seeing as little children, and through a glass, darkly, often not recognising what is there to be seen. However, even when they did not see it, God was still at work providing for them in miraculous ways through people like Elijah—even up to the oil for the Temple Lamps when they took back their Temple in the Intertestamental Period. However, the Israelite Nation had been fully developed, and then handed down to the Tribe of Judah, as declared in Scripture, and now it was time for the next big-ticket item from God. God had taken them from nothing, chosen them as a Family, out of which would produce a Nation; out of which He would choose a Family; who would produce a King like David; from which He Himself would come as a Son/Child (coming as nothing).

> *Who, being in the form of God, thought it not robbery to be equal with God: But* **made Himself of no reputation**, *and took upon Him the form of a servant, and was made in the likeness of men:*

*And being found in fashion as a man, He **humbled Himself**, and **became obedient unto death**, even the death of the cross.*

Philippians 2:6–8

However, because He was in the Form of God, He also brought along some big-ticket items that are the 'Hallmark' of an Awesome God. He healed people, raised them from the dead, cast out demons, and so on for quite a big list of Signs and Wonders. There is a twist to this story, though, He also did them as a man—a mortal created being—just like us! That certainly puts all Signs and Wonders into another ballpark altogether. That means that they are now available to be done on a regular basis by most of us (ordinary people) in some way, and not just some select prophets.

There are a couple of more things that come out of this, and the first one is this: Just as God used special Signs and Wonders to herald the beginning of the Nation of Israel, he also used special Signs and Wonders to Seal them for Himself, in completing His promises to them of A COMING MESSIAH.

The opening and closing acts were of special significance, as any good story should, but it does not stop there. Before I finish on this, I want to mention the second thing that occurred when the **MESSIAH CAME TO EARTH THAT FIRST TIME** (The First Coming), and that it was also the birthing of a NEW Nation of Believers that are to come to God in Praise and Worship, and today, we call them the 'Christians'. Just as Israel was birthed by some big Miracles, then so too was the Christian Nation under God. They were allowed some special giftings to show the Covenants of God in a way that they could understand also. To the young infant Church that was formed then; this was the 'milk' that was to sustain them until the 'meat' was given by way of people like Paul, and John, not to mention the others in their letters (epistles), but ultimately by way of God's Holy Spirit in them. Yes, they would have access to the 'milk' and 'meat' of the Jewish Scriptures, but not everyone would start out with these. Instead, for many, their only contact with these was by way of missionaries, and the signs and wonders they performed. Even the different lifestyles and approaches to situations were to be seen as signs and miracles by many of these people. They were a different identity to the Jews, but they were not so different after all, because they were *'grafted-in'* to the Jewish Covenants by the Shed Blood of The Messiah: Jesus of Nazareth.

This alone has become something of a major stumbling-block to Christians over the years, with Replacement Theology, Displacement Theology, and so many more systems raising their ugly heads above the waters. Even the Missionaries trying to convert the 'Jews First' have produced so many problems, and gave many opportunities for distrust by both sides, and that should never have been the case. We were meant to grow together as one vine:

> *I am the true vine, and My Father is the husbandman. Every branch in Me that beareth not fruit He taketh away: and every branch that beareth fruit, He purgeth it, that it may bring forth more fruit. Now ye are clean through the word which I have spoken unto you. Abide in Me, and I in you. As the branch cannot bear fruit of itself, except it abide in the vine; no more can ye, except ye abide in Me. I am the vine, ye are the branches: He*

> *that abideth in Me, and I in him, the same bringeth forth much fruit: for without Me ye can do nothing.*
>
> John 15:1–5

Yes, this means that the Jews are grafted into the main vine, whom is the Messiah, but it also means that WE ARE GRAFTED INTO THE JEWISH VINE. This is very important to understand, and yet so few seem to know this. Ask any gardener, and they will all tell you, that IF YOU KILL OFF OR REMOVE THE ROOT-STOCK PLANT, THEN THE GRAFT WILL ALSO DIE. You simply cannot have a successful graft if you do not look after the host plant—end of story! As Christians, we need to read and study the Jewish Scriptures (Old Testament), as well as follow what was given for us Gentiles to know and learn (New Testament). Let us never forget that the enemy is not asleep, and trying everything in his power to take people back from God, and he does this with many false signs and wonders, and we are warned of this in:

> *For false Christs and false prophets shall rise, and shall shew signs and wonders, to seduce, if it were possible, even the elect.*
>
> Mark 13:22

Be sober, be vigilant; because your adversary the devil, as a roaring lion, walketh about, seeking whom he may devour.

1 Peter 5:8

I want you to ponder the very battle for our Souls that is going on here. The fact that the Devil relentlessly pursues the ownership of our Souls, and goes to such devious extremes to get them, and the fact that they are of such great importance to God, as to require THE Son of God to come down to die to win our Souls back. This is something which is clearly very, very important to God. Think on this! Did you also notice the Devil goes about as a roaring lion? Just as he comes in the guise of an angel of light, then so does he come in the guise of the Lion of Judah.

That means that there WILL be many signs and wonders performed that are not from God, as we are told in Revelation 13:5–8, 13–17. The ONLY way to discern these is to first contrast and compare with the Written Word of God, and secondly, pray that The Holy Spirit will guide us in all Wisdom and Truth. Truly, we have to remain as grafts to the One True Vine, and not on a cheap copy of one.

> *Verily, verily, I say unto you, He that believeth on Me, the works that I do **shall** he do also; and greater works than these **shall** he do; because I go unto My Father.*
>
> John 14:12
>
> *And these signs **shall** follow them that believe; in My name **shall** they cast out devils; they **shall** speak with new tongues.*
>
> Mark 16:17

Notice that both of these verses are framed in the 'future' context from when they were written (***shall do***—not *already doing*), meaning that it is for a later time; meaning our days of today, or sometime soon for us. Clearly, they are referring to the free use of the Gifts again.

There is another twist that I want to mention now that I have laid down that framework, and it is directly tied in to how Signs and Wonders work.

When we covered the history of the Signs and Wonders over the length of time the Israelite Nation was in existence, we saw a clear pattern; one which will happen to us in exactly the same way, and for the very same reasons. The pattern is this: a burst as we are formed, then some along the way to keep our hopes up, and then a burst as things are being fulfilled. So, we should see a burst as we are formed as an infant church, some miracles along the way, but not as an ongoing daily thing, and then a burst as things come to completion—**THE MESSIAH'S RETURN.**

To further complicate the matter, it is not because of *us* that this happens, but is still directly tied back the Israelite Nation and what happens to it. The graft is still very reliant on the host plant! When the host plant is doing well, then the graft prospers also.

In another of my works (to be published later as part of this *Foundation Stones* series) on *Time Frames in Prophecy*, I state this:

> *There is yet another aspect of Time-Frames that no-one seems to look at, and that is the historical relationships between 'God directing the people', and 'man directing people'. Take a look at just when the Shekinah Glory was given to the Jews via the Ark of the Covenant, and*

> *when it disappeared from history, and put these on your calendar. Then look at the rise and fall of Man's Religions and compare them to the previous dates, and you will see an arrest in the spreading of these lesser systems whilst the Shekinah Glory was around, and a massive blow-out of them starting around the globe within six months of the Shekinah Glory/Ark disappearing from our grasp. This blow-out continues right up until the Devil System is fully in place with the Son of Perdition in the Tribulation, and is there as a warning for us to avoid.*

With this, we can clearly see that there is a correlation between the relationship of the Jews with God, and acting out on their experience of God's Miracles and Signs for them. We also saw a mention of a 'Lack of Vision' ('chazon') being mentioned in our Scriptures. Go to the first book of Samuel:

> *And the child Samuel ministered unto the LORD before Eli. And the word of the LORD was precious in those days; there was no open vision.*
>
> 1 Samuel 3:1

What is Prophecy?

Yet again, in a future publication in this series, we will note this about *the Jews:*

For the Jews today, there is no 'Pillar of Cloud' by day, nor 'Shekinah Flame' by night. (The Shekinah Glory was seen to depart the Temple in 66 AD, where it moved to the Mount of Olives for 3½ years, before disappearing [69 AD] just before the Romans came and destroyed the Temple). They have no Altars, no Sacrifices, and no Priesthood as in former days. They observe the 'Passover', but no Pascal Lamb is slain. They keep the 'Great Day of Atonement', but no blood is shed to make reconciliation for sin. All sacrifices and oblations have ceased. They have no King, no Judges, no Prophets, and no Inspired Writers. The 'Urim' and 'Thummin' give no Divine Token. The Word of God is precious, but there is little 'Open Vision'. [Many don't even believe in their own God, or even their Scriptures anymore]. Their Last Great Prophet was the 'Man of Galilee', but Him they rejected. It seems as if the Jews are

> *a forgotten people, and yet their survival is a story that defies logic, for they didn't just fade away like the other nations that were destroyed; they've come back from the dead. Hosea 3:4, Luke 21:24 and Romans 11:25–26 foretell this phase of Israel's life and the reason is given in Romans 11:1–2, Ezekiel 37:21–22, and also Jeremiah 30:10-11, Amos 9:14–15, Isaiah 11:11–12, and so on, all purport to Israel's Restoration.*

The problem of not having some 'Open Vision' still remains today. Both Jews and Christians suffer from this, and yet the story is not over yet. Now, let us bring you more up to date with what has been happening historically with the Jews since the destruction of the Temple. The Jews were dispersed and their Temple destroyed. Talk about blockage to the flow of things. They became citizens of various countries around the world, with new pressures on their Jewishness that they had not encountered before.

As a result, over time, their Jewishness retreated from studying all of their Scrolls, right back to just the *Torah* (the first five Books of Moses), the

Mishna, and the *Talmud* (Commentaries and Oral Traditions), and even these latter works were not studied in any great detail for so many.

The bulk of the *Tanakh* (Old Testament) became largely ignored by so many Jewish Scholars. The *Torah* is the source of Divine Commandments that are at the heart of Jewishness, and read each Sabbath. However, of what use was stories of kings and prophets when they lived under strange laws and traditions, without any political power of their own? They even bought into the lie that the 'God of Old' was a vindictive, wrathful God— entirely unloving to them at all.

Even Christians bought into this lie, and only accepted the Old Testament under pressure, because it held no religious value. The Hebrew Bible was even considered to be a Jewish Conspiracy! What incredible deception had come on them all?

During the time of Hitler, this view took on an even greater role, which continues to this day, with many even trying to remove the Old Testament from having any input at all, by both Jews and Christians. This marginalisation of the Jewish History and Prophets continues on with growing impetus as we move closer into the Times of the Antichrist.

However, there is a big stumbling-block in the road for these theories, and it is the very fact that the Jewish People have again entered into their own land; are again reading their Historical and Prophetic Scrolls, and are again starting to realise a new 'vision' for their land (the Clarity developing around God's Will).

What is really interesting is the new upsurge of the Jews finding the scrolls of their history and prophets now that they are under attack from outside their land. This completely mirrors what is happening in the Christian Realms, as the Gifts of Old are finding a new 're-emergence' in action. I want you to take a look at the parallel time-lines, for they are side-by-side all along the path back to God for all of us. Israel is again experiencing the Miracles of God (including the fulfillment of them again occupying their land despite all odds against it), and finding Grace where they thought they had none (despite the increased attacks from the Devil). Christianity is similarly experiencing miracles again, and it points to the fulfillment of the very same prophecies that were untaught for so long.

The revival of the Nation of Israel led to a revival in the study of the Hebrew Scriptures, in both Jewish and Christian circles. The Biblical stories of kings and prophets, which had seemed so irrelevant, are once again essential texts. Simply put, the greatest miracle that we see happening is the regaining of 'the vision' that is so important.

> *And it shall come to pass afterward, that I will pour out My spirit upon all flesh; and your sons and your daughters shall prophesy, your old men shall dream dreams, your young men shall see visions.*
>
> Joel 2:28

Another facet of the End Times is the 'Unsealing' of the books which Daniel was told to seal up. God will use those who are called, and gifted accordingly, to open up these things for God's Church to know, and to follow.

Clearly though, this time is NOT the end of prophecy, for we see the outpouring of so much dreaming and visions! That means that there is still more to come before we see the finality of it all, and, while the Word of God clearly tells us that it will be a Time of Great Tribulation, it will also be an exciting time, where we will get to enter into The Kingdom of God. It will be a time like no other, in all of history, where we get to see the completeness of evil being employed against God and His Goodness. It, in itself, will be a fulfillment of part of Prophecy, but that there is still more to go before we cross the finish line.

I do wonder if these temporary gifts will not be needed in Eternity, because all of them will *be the normal* for ALL of us in our glorified bodies—no-one without any of them? Nothing special or notable about them at all for us as individuals, for everyone will display all of them as a natural part of us, PLUS more!

This has been a journey, and yet it is still not complete, for we have not mentioned the last chapter of the pattern God has put in place for all of this to occur. It starts with our Resurrection, and goes all the way to Eternal life in the Celestial City of God. This chapter will include some more very big-ticket items, like the Second Death, and the New Heavens and New Earth. THIS is the full-stop to the need for anything else (like Prophecy), for we will need nothing under God, for He has promised that we will live in His Increase, as His Children. I can only hope and pray that you take the steps to enter in for yourself; to live in your own mansion of the most spectacular design and materials; to explore the universe as well as inhabit it, in the Peace of God.

> *He which testifieth these things saith,*
> *Surely I come quickly. Amen.*
> **Even so, come, Lord Jesus.**
>
> Revelation 22:20
>
> *The grace of our Lord Jesus Christ*
> *be with you all. Amen.*
>
> Revelation 22:21
>
> AMEN

BY THE SAME AUTHOR

This is the first in a series of books on understanding Biblical Prophecy. The next volume will be *Beresheet: The Prophecy of Creation*. Following up will be various subjects including *The Jews, Gentiles, Israel, and the Church; Calendars and Timelines; Some Specific Prophecies; Revelation and the End Times;* and various other titles covering subjects as diverse as *God is the Same and God with Logic, Spiritual Truths as Prophecy, Verification in the Word with some Examples of Fulfilment, Language Used and Unusual Descriptions*, and *Progressive Revelation*.

Bishop Dighton has also been a co-author of a Military Manual on a piece of VC Ordnance, titled *A Diabolical Device*; this through the Navy Sea Power Centre. In addition there are various articles, papers, and pieces over the years, including those in the anthologies *Palette of Grace* and *Symphony of Grace*.

Availalbe via Amazon

The Covenant of Salt

This is a Bible Study done back in 2018 on a subject that is rarely taught these days, and yet it is still a Covenant between us and God. I believe it is good to know something about what, how, and Who we believe, and are covenanted into.

The Rock: A Bible Study

As Our Lord and Saviour is 'The Rock of Ages', I did a study on all different aspects of how this could play out in our lives, including a list of all the Bible passages regarding rock/s and stone/s for you to think about yourself.

www.ingramcontent.com/pod-product-compliance
Lightning Source LLC
Chambersburg PA
CBHW052054070526
44584CB00017B/2177